Minoan Crete

LIFE IN ANCIENT LANDS
Edited by Edward Bacon

Minoan Crete

H. E. L. Mellersh

Evans Brothers Limited London

This book was designed and produced by George Rainbird Ltd,
2 Hyde Park Place, London W2,
for Evans Brothers Limited,
Montague House, Russell Square, London WC1.
The text was filmset in Great Britain by
Cox and Sharland Ltd, Southampton.
The book was printed and bound in Hungary

7/5052

CONTENTS

COLOUR PLATES

FOREWORD

The world as we know it is a man-made world. Hardly any part of the habitable globe is unaffected by man's activity; even some of the parts which are uninhabitable were made so by man. And man himself is very largely a man-made creature: his habits, his thoughts, his memory, his aspirations are the modified sum of his ancestors' experiences.

All men are brothers, say the missionary and the idealist. True, but there is more to it than that: all men, living and dead since the beginning of time, are our brothers; and all history is family history. The Magdalenian artist of 17,000 years ago who decorated the caves of Lascaux with bulls and horses, the Cretan who applauded the bull-leapers, the Egyptian who drew funny hippopotamuses on pieces of stone, the boy Inca who triumphed in the initiation tests, the Etruscans who delighted so frankly in wine, women and song—these are as real to us, as near to us and as sustaining to us as, at any rate, some of those who live in our own street, village, town. Or they can be.

Aristotle said that the object of poetry was pleasure. And when he used these words, he doubtless used them in the widest possible sense: poetry, to include the full range of man's creative imagination; pleasure, to encompass everything from the baby's first chuckle to the philosopher's cry of delight at apprehending a new facet of truth. Education and the pursuit of knowledge have two objectives: pleasure and power. And of these the greater is pleasure: power is transitory, pleasure is permanent.

If these books enable anyone to pass an examination, to secure a job or to dominate a competitor or friend, they will have served a purpose of a sort. Their main objective, however, is to increase the sum of human pleasure, to enlarge the circle of friendship, love and knowledge, and to present a picture of life.

Life in ancient Crete has a special fascination. Though one of the greatest and most distinct of ancient civilizations, practically nothing was known of it—even that it had existed—until the present century. It is, in a sense, the complete creation of the archaeologist's spade and the scholar's detective imagination. It has no literature; until a few years ago, its written records were undecipherable. Even now, when thanks to the brilliant work of Ventris and Chadwick those records are transcribed, they turn out to be little more than duty-rosters and the lists of quarter-masters and tax-collectors.

And yet, the brilliance, the luxury, the oddity and gaiety of Minoan Crete are now manifest like that phrase of Sterne's "the world of fashion running at the ring of pleasure". Sterne was writing of Paris; and it was not by accident that Sir Arthur Evans called one of the fresco portraits of girls he found at Knossos La Belle Parisienne. Life at Knossos was lively, sophisticated, modish—a good thousand years before Pericles.

7

It had its tragedies, its decadence, its final disaster, its disappearance — but this is true of every civilization that has ever been. Man's societies seem to carry within them the seeds of their own destruction. Everything has its term; and though lives and civilizations are not for ever, they are still rich in delight or the potential of delight; and few are more delightful than Minoan Crete.

EDWARD BACON

Chapter One

A CIVILIZATION ALMOST FORGOTTEN

A people who have been called the first Europeans, a people rediscovered in the twentieth century, a people whose art, architecture, customs and dress surprised the archaeologists and the whole world: these were the Minoans of Bronze Age Crete.

Their very name reflects the unexpectedness of their discovery. We do not know what the ancient Cretans called themselves. Conventional history had called them nothing, for such history had not considered their existence. Their fabled king, or their line of kings, had been called Minos: Minoans they have therefore become. It is as if the Egyptians had been called "Pharaohans" or the Hittites "Suppiluliamans"—a resounding name, if difficult—or the English Alfredians or Offans. However, one name is as good as another so long as all are agreed upon it. The name "Minoan" serves to remind us that our knowledge of these people depends almost entirely on the myth plus the spade, on what the classical folklorist and the twentieth century archaeologist have preserved or discovered. Minoan writing does exist, and has been at least half deciphered, but nowhere yet has the name of the land or the people appeared; if it ever does appear, in all probability the experts will quarrel over its exact spelling and pronunciation and will be forced, in sheer desperation, to stick to the name that Sir Arthur Evans, in his self-assured wisdom, invented.

The Minoans, then, of Bronze Age Crete. They lived in, they managed to create, a civilization by all appearances gay and pleasure-loving, sophisticated and safe, materially prosperous yet permeated by religious ideas that appear to us strange and must have been by them enthusiastically accepted and passionately believed in. They wore clothes that an early viewer of their frescoes, thinking no doubt of the Naughty Nineties, called Parisian (plate 8). They made of the bull a portentous symbol; yet they played with the bull. They evolved for themselves a remarkably modern plumbing system. They laid a debt for all time upon the early Greeks, for the civilizing influence that they exerted upon them; and legend has it that they laid a tribute upon them at the time of Theseus, for, no doubt, exerting their pacifying powers in the Mediterranean to all the lesser peoples' benefit. How all this could have been achieved needs some explanation.

First, the Minoans lived on an island, and that island was in the Mediterranean: not for nothing did the world's earliest civilizations cluster round this great inland sea. The climate of Crete was beautiful, and still is beautiful; the land was more fertile than it is now; the sun shone but was not a burden, not a burden that is to say to the bronzed natives who had grown up under it. In more prosaic language, the Cretans lived in a temperate zone; their island lies, as on a bed, straight but warm, on that line on the map which we call latitude 35 degrees. And New York lies at 41 degrees, Paris at 49 degrees, London at 52 degrees, Oslo at 60 degrees.

And Crete is very much in the midst of the Mediterranean, with all the advantage that a surround of sea can give in defeating climatic extremes. It *is* an island—which in itself has great significance. First of all, an island that cannot be reached by a boatman who is unwilling to fare forth and lose sight of land is not likely to become humanly populated until men have achieved some nautical skill and daring, in fact until neolithic times. Crete is one such island, at least it appears to be so from the archaeologist's evidence. That fact has perhaps no very great significance; but to have to suffer nothing from the dead, conservative hand of the palaeolithic hunter, the Old Stone Age savage set in his ways for not thousands but tens of thousands of years, may have been a not inconsiderable asset. Islands, however, have a more obvious potential advantage. They are isolated, they are sea-girt: as Shakespeare had it, they possess the sea "as a moat defensive to a house". Only one thing, but a very necessary thing, is needed to make this defence a real one: those on the island must have control of the seas around them, for otherwise they will become no more than a target for attack, by the invader and the pirate. Until their fall, the Minoans had that command of the sea.

They were well placed for it and ideally placed for that which gives wealth and power, the exercise of trade.

Trade is the life blood of early civilizations, as it is indeed of all civilizations, though with the early ones it is a more romantic, a more dangerous, adventurous, stimulating, thought-widening affair. Those people of the early world who indulged in trade were the ones who immensely increased their material wealth, and not only by the mere fact of exchange but even more so by the stimulus to production that advantageous ex-

Crete, centrally positioned in the eastern Mediterranean

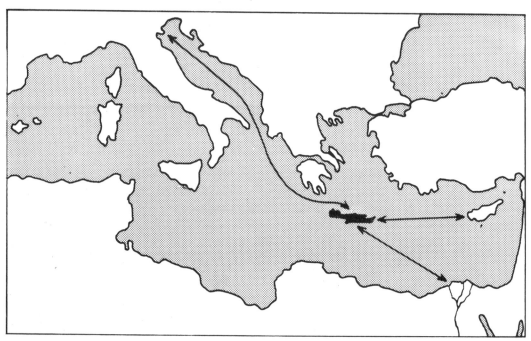

change imparts. They increased too their imaginative heritage and the activity of the cells of their brains by the exchange of ideas and the increase of experience that the profession of voyager and merchant-adventurer gave. Crete found herself particularly well placed for trade when the Bronze Age arrived. Not only was there the increase generally in the need to trade and travel and prospect which the insistent demand for the precious metals caused; not only that but, more importantly, more luckily for the Minoan, his little boat-shaped island was pretty well exactly on the spot where the lines of the great trade routes crossed. Copper came from Cyprus and copper and tin from as far afield as the Erzgebirge or Ore Mountains of what is now Czechoslovakia. Their wealth created demand for luxuries, or, to use a more meaningful word for the times, things of beauty. Amber from Scandinavia joined the overland route and arrived with copper and tin at the head of the Adriatic Sea. Egypt had much gold. Perhaps even so early, brave men penetrated beyond the Pillars of Hercules where the Phoenicians later traded; certainly they reached beyond the Hellespont and to the Asia Minor and Lebanon coasts, to exchange with the Scythians and the Hittites and the Babylonians and perhaps even with the distant east. Draw lines north and south, and east and west, from modern Cairo to Trieste, from Cyprus to Gibraltar, and you can hardly avoid crossing Crete.*

But if the ancient people of Crete were faced with the opportunity to achieve prosperity and greatness, that opportunity was not an easy one and they would not necessarily possess the strength of character to seize it. The people, however, who could seize a real bull by the horns were not likely to be unable to seize a metaphorical one. They were both a tough and a lively people. Heredity and environment had inevitably shaped them.

All lands shape the people who live in them. Whoever had been the first neolithic immigrants, they found a rugged, mountainous country where only the valleys were fertile (plate 1). Very fertile those would be, but there would not be too many of them. Where now the mountains are a bare, pale-grey granite almost to their bases where in a straggling way the olive trees begin, then they would be clothed to near their heights with forests. But though a forest gives timber it needs much human energy with the axe if any of it is to be cleared to give grazing for beasts or foothold for olive tree or vine. Then mountains tend to isolate the valleys and the people in them, as they do, even more so, in Greece, a land that Crete much resembles. Inhabitants of such lands are liable to grow not only hardy but independent and individualistic.

Greeks and Minoans were not, however, of the same stock. The Minoans were a more ancient and indigenous people, indigenous that is to say to the Mediterranean, much alike no doubt those people whom the Greeks, coming in from the north, met and called the Pelasgians: dark people, and little and lithe. Ethnology has been able to give these people no better name than "Mediterraneans". Sometimes they have been called Dark-Whites, sometimes Iberians though that presupposes that when later the

* This is a point made by Gustav Glotz in his book, *The Aegean Civilization* (Kegan Paul, 1925). He adds that Knossos is the same distance from Troy as another ancient Cretan port, Zakro, is from the Nile delta. Zakro has been recently excavated by Dr N. Platon.

type spread north and west it came only from Spain. They are not Semitic. But they are dark. They are essentially long or narrow headed, dolicho-cephalic, having a skull long from front to rear when viewed from above. It is a type often seen in the Mediterranean though not now much in Greece nor very much in Crete itself; surprisingly it may turn up in England, among the Cornish for instance, and at Avebury museum in Wiltshire may be seen a child's skull of those first British farmers, the Windmill Hill people, who did indeed come from the Mediterranean. Besides being pronouncedly narrow it is a small and delicate skull.

Small therefore and small boned were the Cretans, with narrow waists but good broad shoulders — a neat and vivid and graceful people.

Chapter Two

BRONZE AGE PEOPLE

Really the Bronze Age is an astounding age, an age that has been proved so much more rich and successful and long-lived than any historian at the beginning of this century would have dared to believe.

The Minoan civilization is essentially of the Bronze Age; and in seeking to set the Minoans in their historical as well as their geographical setting—indeed in seeking to understand them at all and to realize them as men and women who once lived and loved and thought and felt—we must be able to appreciate what existence in the Bronze Age signified.

It signified of course much more than the fact that by now somebody, or bodies, had learnt to fuse copper with about ten per cent of tin to create a metal that could be cast

"A man of the earth": a scene from the Hagia Triada Harvester Cup

and forged and was hard and handsome and durable. The Bronze Age not only came directly after the later or New Stone Age, the Neolithic; it also inherited from it, it was in fact a rich extension of it. And Neolithic Man had emerged from being a mere hunter and had become a farmer; he was therefore a man of the earth, earthy, and earthy in a much deeper sense than that he was a little muddy of hand or dusty of clothes. He had become a working partner with Mother Earth; and this senior partner of his was a pretty potent person, not to say mysterious person, who needed to be propitiated with sacrifice and to be worshipped.

This is certainly not the place to attempt a resumé of Frazer's *Golden Bough*. The point we are attempting to make is simply that the Bronze Age man, any Bronze Age man anywhere, was the son of neolithic man and was therefore essentially a religious person, meaning by "religious" all that goes with belief in magic and sacrifice and symbolism and propitiation and omen. Economic Man does not yet exist, any more than does Scientific Man. Only Religious Man exists. Such a one is indeed as anxious as any modern to live fully and to live well, as passionate and as wilful in his desires. But he will think in totally different terms when it comes to implementing those desires. His prosperity he will consider as bound up with the prosperity of his nation or people, governed as they no doubt are by the king who is also priest to the goddess, Mother Earth. Be he merchant or sailor, landowner or craftsman or peasant — and there is not much else that he can be — he will think in that way. At the highest his desires will be for prestige and power and honour and pleasure and the possession of beautiful things; at the lowest it will be for a full belly and the salvation from war and plague and such unhappy demon-

Left. "The possession of beautiful things": a rhyton from Psira

Right. Charging bull fresco (restored); from the portico of the North Propylon, Knossos

strations of the powers of Nature as flood and tempest and that devastating eruption of the earth which the Minoans are likely to have called the Roaring of the Great Bull—the sort of bull that is depicted here.

So we bring ourselves back to the Minoans, from the Bronze Age man in general to the same in particular. The Minoan was typical of his time and must have thought typically. No doubt the pregnant girl did indeed go to the equivalent of a clinic; but it was a holy cave she went to, to present her votive offering to that particular personification of the great Mother Goddess who took care of the likes of her. The merchant-skipper did not fail to insure against loss at sea; but he went, most likely, to an expert on omens—omens of the flight of birds perhaps, since Minoans thought much in terms of the symbolism of birds—and this expert would tell him when and when not to sail.

In one thing the Minoans were not only typical of their age but outstanding; in another they were conspicuously untypical, at least until near their end. The first is wealth and the second is war. The Bronze Age was an age of wealth and much-sought-after wealth—no contemporary ruler for instance thought it beneath his dignity to cadge for Egypt's gold. Crete had no gold, but she had her industrious peasants and her brilliant artists to supply the goods which her adventurous merchant-sailors would exchange for gold. As for war, we have observed that Crete was a well-protected island. There could have been internal strife, but there is no specific sign of it. Only when the Bronze Age as a whole was becoming chronically warlike, was indeed beginning the process of committing suicide, does Crete, as we shall see, suffer if not from war at least from the rule of the war lord.

B.C.	EUROPE	EGYPT	THE AEGEAN
2100	Windmill Hill people in Britain	Middle Kingdom begins	
2000	Neolithic Age	Dynasty XI	Entry of Aryan-speakers
	First Stonehenge	Story of Sinuhe	
1900			
	The megalith builders	Sesostris III	
1800			
		Second Inter-mediate Period	Rise of Mycenaeans
1700	Entry of Bronze Beaker People	Hyksos invasion and rule	
1600	Last Stonehenge		Shaft graves at Mycenae
		New Kingdom and Empire	
1500	Wessex culture in Britain Bronze Age prosperity		Thera eruption(?)
		Tuthmosis III	Theseus (?)
1400			
		Akhenaten Tutankhamen	
1300	Spread of Battle Axe people (Aryan?) to north-west	Rameses II	Height of Mycenaean Age
		Exodus of Jews	
			Agamemnon (?)
1200			
		Rameses III	
1100			
		Decline of Egypt	Dorians and "Dark Age"
1000	The Celts		

CHART

CRETE	ASIA MINOR & PALESTINE	MESOPOTAMIA	B.C.
Early Minoan II	Troy V		2100
Early Minoan III	Entry of Aryan-speakers	Third Dynasty of Ur	2000
Middle Minoan I			
	Assyrian traders		1900
		Abraham	
Middle Minoan II	Troy VI		1800
		Hammurabi	
Destruction of first palaces	Rise of Hittites Hyksos	Hittites in Babylon	1700
Middle Minoan III			
	Hittites conquer Mitanni	Kassites in Babylon	1600
Late Minoan I			1500
Entry of Mycenaeans and Late Minoan II			
Destruction of second palaces	Battle of Megiddo	Rise of Assyria	1400
			1300
Late Minoan III	First use of iron	End of Kassites	
Dorians begin to enter	Moses		1200
	Fall of Troy (VIIA)	Tiglath Pileser I	1100
Sub-Minoan Dorian dominion complete	Hebrew Judges Philistines David Phoenicians		1000

Sir Arthur Evans, painted against a fresco
background by Sir W. B. Richmond

18

We need a little history and a few dates. The Bronze Age did not of course come into being all over the world at the same time. But curiously enough it does seem to last a usually prosperous thousand years whenever and wherever it begins; and that thousand years in the Mediterranean very roughly is the last quarter of the third millennium B.C. and the first three quarters of the second — perhaps usually a little longer on each side. Minoans existed of course both before and after those dates. But in the afterwards the island was steadily ceasing to be Minoan; and as for neolithic Crete she was as it were a child, only yet preparing to be a beautiful lady — a slow process where nations are concerned.

The time chart will show a little of what was happening in the rest of the civilized world during this thousand years and more. At its beginning the world's two earliest and greatest river-valley civilizations were already well established, while in the Indus valley that rather grim and regimented culture had but lately begun. In its middle Abraham did his great trek from Ur of the Chaldees, Hammurabi gave his laws to the Sumerians and barbarian western Europe began to feel the pressure, or the benefit, of the people from the Mediterranean who knew both bronze and the way to build very greatly in stone. Egypt suffered her second relapse, called most inadequately by the historians an "intermediate period", and became fertilized by the bedouin blood of the Hyksos. Then towards the end of the period all is movement and action and change. New names of peoples appear. Assyrians, Hittites, Mycenaeans. Egypt becomes a warlike empire-seeker. The traffic of men and ideas is now not only outwards from the seat of the great civilizations but also inwards and from the north. Since Minoan Crete is greatly affected by part of this movement we shall return to it in the last chapter.

We need one other historical framework, that of the Bronze Age Minoans themselves. It is that invented by Sir Arthur Evans, and is based on the major changes in Egypt, from her so-called Old, to Middle, to New Kingdoms. As Evans is the re-discoverer of ancient Crete, and as Egypt was likely in her early days to have been her chief mentor, it is doubly fitting that it should be used, as it still is, though the dates have been somewhat altered. Here it is, as now usually given:

Early Minoan Period: 2500 B.C. to 1950 B.C.
Middle Minoan Period: 1950 B.C. to 1550 B.C.
Late Minoan Period: 1550 B.C. to 1100 B.C.

Each of these periods is in fact usually broken down into three, and then — for simplicity in writing if not in thought — abbreviated into initials, so that we get for instance LMIII, which is the last part of the Late Minoan Period (and incidentally more different from LMII than LMI is different from MMIII). These sub-divisions are shown on the chart, but we will try to avoid them in the text. There is in fact something of a growing tendency to use a quite different nomenclature, as being more appropriate to Crete's own history and not to Egyptian. This uses the divisions, Prepalatial, Protopalatial, Neopalatial and Postpalatial, depending on whether that particularly significant aspect of Minoan life, her great palaces, were not yet built, were built in their early form, had reached their renewed and final form, or had come to ruin. They are usually shown the same in date as in Evans's revised framework, except that the first division is shown at about 1700 and not 1950 B.C. Neo and Postpalatial correspond to Late Minoan II and III.

We are concerned with Minoan life, however, and not primarily with her history.

True Minoan greatness lies well within the given span, say 1900 to 1400 B.C. Her full flowering, the times with which we are all familiar — the times of bull-leapers and snake goddesses and splendid ladies in flounced dresses, of fabled Theseus and Ariadne and the Minotaur, of splendid palaces, efficient drains and imaginative art — all this is confined within the periods called Middle Minoan III to Late Minoan II or, if it is preferred and more simply, Neopalatial, the seventeenth, sixteenth and fifteenth centuries B.C. As a near enough approximation, we are looking back over a span of three and a half millennia. In terms of human generations it perhaps does not seem quite so long: say a hundred to a hundred and fifty.*

*Professor L. R. Palmer has lately been challenging Sir Arthur Evans's dating. His recommendations are not followed in this book; but there is some discussion of them in Chapter Ten.

Chapter Three

LIFE IN THE ORDINARY

It is a natural and common cry, the cry against the historian's apparently too great preoccupation with the upper stratum of society: "tell us about the *common* people!" In truth however this is somewhat a misconceived demand, and perhaps the more so as one goes back in time. The common people of the Bronze Age must have lived in much the same way all over the Mediterranean, and a fairly dull, uneventful, unprogressive, un-significant, tied-to-the-earth existence it must have been. It is a noble sentiment to feel sympathy for these common people, but a mistaken idea that history lies with them. Largely, history rode rough-shod over them.

None the less, such people probably constituted ninety per cent of the population. However rich the Mediterranean Bronze Age grew by means of trade seasoned with a little piracy, the goods exchanged had to be produced, as did also the wherewithal to feed the hungry mouths; and with no machine to augment and magnify the human muscle beyond the bow-and-arrow and the lumbering ox-plough, the great majority of the population must have been engaged in hard and sweaty peasant labour.

Very many of these people would undoubtedly have been serfs or slaves, tied to their jobs to a greater or lesser extent. At least, however, there seems some ground for thinking that the underdog in ancient Crete was not treated like a cur. There is the evidence of the Harvester Cup (see pages 13 and 22). On it men are shown in procession back from the fields, or in harvest thanksgiving, and they are singing lustily and happily. This of course is only the artist's idea; but it is at least possible, likely even, that he was portraying what he had seen.

The laws of a land, their efficacy and their humanity, are another factor governing the lot of the common man, be he peasant or serf or slave. There has been discovered as yet no code of Cretan law as was discovered the Code of Hammurabi, King of Babylon at the time when Minoan greatness was beginning. Nevertheless, Minos has a great fabled reputation as a lawgiver; and the fact that he is, with a blatant inconsistency, also portrayed as a rapacious monster need not necessarily make us discount the kindlier representation: folklore is often ambivalent, and the monstrous reputation was in all probability the result of fear and lack of understanding on the part of jealous subjugated peoples. Aristotle, relying on who knows what record, but a scientific and eminently fair-minded man, credits ancient Crete with a particularly enlightened ruler and says that the Cretans gave to their slaves the same institutions as their own—which was more than Hammurabi did. He adds however that they forbade their slaves either the practice of gymnastic exercises or the possession of arms: they must be neither too fit nor too forceful, on the whole a reasonable precaution.

Evidence rather more slender that the common man lived in Crete a happier life than most of his contemporaries comes from another of the classic Greeks—who if they were living a thousand years away from the Minoans were at least over a couple of thousand years nearer to them than ourselves. Plato did indeed plan his ideal commonwealth of Atlantis not in the Mediterranean but beyond the Pillars of Hercules. But the Greeks' "Isle of the Dead" was always put beyond these pillars, and it does seem as if Plato were intentionally mixing a mythical place with what he knew of a real one. He also significantly traces knowledge of Atlantis to the tales of an Egyptian priest, and Egyptians were the most likely to know about Crete. Discounting therefore a subsequently sunken continent in the Atlantic—which if it ever existed is not likely to have done so, the geologists tell us, short of several million years ago—we are left with the probability of Crete, or at least of memories of ancient Crete, being the model for Plato's ideal commonwealth. Atlantis was rich and powerful and delighted in wonderful palaces; its shipping was master of the seas; there was a ritual of bull sacrifice and a chasing of the bull "without weapons but with staves and nooses"; the laws of the land were justly administered by a great prince. All in all, the description fits Crete very well.

Another legend does not give quite so idyllic a picture though it does suggest an efficient central control. Daedalus, the engineer—he is the great mythical *inventive* figure for Crete as Imhotep was for Egypt—came to the aid of King Minos when the latter found his land with its long coastline and separated valleys difficult to control. Daedalus invented the first robot, who three times a day patrolled the land. His name was Talos, he was a bronze giant, and fire spouted from his mouth: the world's first known policeman, even if wonderful, was not exactly likeable.

So much for legend. Men, however common, can enjoy the natural benefits of a country and must endure its disadvantages. The climate of Crete is indeed beautiful and must also have been so three and four thousand years ago; there may be heavy rains in autumn and early spring, and dry and dust-raising winds can blow; but mostly the sun shines, and brings out happily the warm scents from the green plants upon which it shines. Cypress and oak and fir and cedar were the island's chief trees; and, as now, poppy and iris and anemone flowered. Bees hummed and butterflies flitted; and by the fact that they have been so lovingly portrayed their happy presence must have been appreciated. In the heat the cicada, the giant grasshopper, that however flits like a small, rather drunken bat between the trees, no doubt sent out its monotonous chant. I have watched, on the terrace of the guest house above the ruins of Phaistos, a little Cretan boy being teased by having one of these lazy, clumsy, unresistant insects placed in his hair; perhaps the same somewhat insensitive but harmless sport was also indulged in by the Minoans.

But what was the typical peasant doing, how was he living? What crops did he grow? Was he typically shepherd, or ploughman; or, in modern language, market-gardener; or fisherman, or even hunter?

Alas, there is no simple answer, for there can have been no typical peasant—a fact that ties up with the suggestion already made that such a country as Crete breeds rugged individuality. The other two sites of the world's earliest civilizations are Sumeria and Egypt, and those were both river-valley civilizations, where silt and mud gave phenomenal fertility, and phenomenal dullness. The Minoans managed to be a very good third in

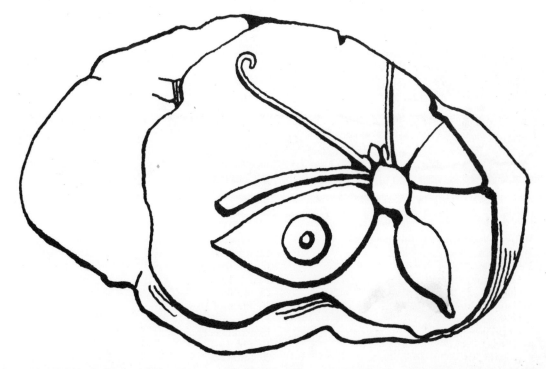

Left. Peasants singing; a scene from the Hagia Triada Harvester Cup

Above. Butterfly on a clay seal, from Hagia Triada

the race to civilization, and without the advantage of any vast, flat river valley; they must therefore have been able to fall back on some compensating advantage: in one word, variety.

Nowadays on the southern coast of Crete one can buy home-grown bananas and watch men, as late as October, putting into the warm ground tomato plants with no other protection than wattle wind-breaks. But in this same island a few hours' journey will take one from this warm plain from which the swallows do not fly in winter to mountain heights where there is perpetual snow; and intermediately there will be traversed upland plateaus where corn grows well and in summer the sheep and cattle graze.

This imagined journey affords an opportunity to ask the reader to glance at the island's geography. Superficially Crete looks from the map like an island with one continuous backbone of mountain; but though it is true that no route from north to south will be flat or easy yet the backbone is in fact divided into three mountain ranges. These are Leuka or the White Mountains in the west, Ida in the centre and Dicte in the east, each range rising above 6,000 feet. All must have been clothed in Minoan times with forest to not far from their peaks, and the surprising fact that the west of the island yields very little trace indeed of early occupation leads to the belief that in that area the trees were never cleared and the Minoans disappeared before the forest ever did. Mount Ida, twice the height of Snowdon, is with its distinctive wide-spaced double peak a landmark for the whole of central and southern Crete, the palace of Phaistos included. It is a reputed birthplace of Zeus. Dicte is also a reputed birthplace of Zeus, only rather more so; and between these two ranges the isolated mountain of Juktas, visible from Knossos, holds the grave of Zeus and in addition shows in its outline

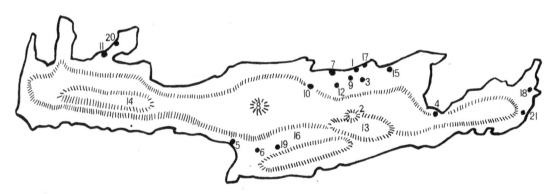

Map of Crete, showing the principal sites

1 Amnisos	11 Khania
2 Mt Dicte	12 Knossos
3 Eilythyia	13 Lasithi uplands
4 Gournia	14 Leuka Mts
5 Hagia Galene	15 Mallia
6 Hagia Triada	16 Plain of Messara
7 Heraklion	17 Nirou Khani
8 Mt Ida	18 Palaikastro
9 Isopata	19 Phaistos
10 Mt Juktas	20 Suda Bay
	21 Zakros

24

the recumbent profile of that bearded god. All of which leads one to suppose that the Minoans were imaginative, and, like the Israelites, looked up to the hills from whence would come their help. More practically, Dicte in the east provides the most extensive of the upland plateaus, Lasithi; and south of Ida is the island's largest and longest fertile valley, the plain of Messara, greater in extent than any similar valley of the Peloponnese, the horse-breeding vale of Argos included.

Crete then, more wooded and less desiccated than it is now, was blessed with fertility at different levels and climates; it could grow a variety of things if it wished, and it could grow the celebrated trio of the ancient Mediterranean world, corn, grapes and olives, supremely well. In practice Crete probably did not wish to grow much more than these three: corn in the flat uplands, the gnarled olive, hardy once established, growing up the lower flanks of the mountains wherever the forest was cleared, vines in serried ranks in the valleys. Those must have been the staple products of Minoan Crete, creating their own typical landscape, demanding their own particular toll of human toil—and anyone who has seen the peasants of modern Crete or Greece tend the ground beneath the olive trees, coaxing towards the roots all the moisture available, will know that even the least obvious work-producer of these three is an insistent one.

The Minoan peasant was also a shepherd and at times a swineherd. The swineherd let his beasts roam the forest, the goatherd watched, unmoved, his charges proceed with the early stages of denuding his island of that same forest by gnawing the bark from trees, and for the rest no doubt let them eat wherever they could—unless perhaps he was driving them across his neighbour's land when, as nowadays, he may have taken the

Seal showing a goat drawing a carriage

precaution of fitting them with muzzles. As for the shepherd of sheep, he would, again as now, take his flocks to the plateaus in the summer and down to the lowland pastures nearer to the villages in the winter.

A fisherman the Minoan must have been; for his forefathers had arrived in boats, and the sea was all around him. Murex, the sea mussel, would give purple dye as well as food, and there would be a multitude of small squid to be caught. For the fowler there would be pigeon and partridge, and, as migratory visitors, duck and quail and snipe and woodcock. For the hunter there were deer, at least in the western forests, the native wild goat or ibex, and the splendid Cretan bull.

There are two things to say about the hunter however. One is that, after palaeolithic times, when every man had been a hunter, the exercise seems everywhere to have become a royal one, or at least an aristocratic one. If the peasant was a hunter we may imagine him a poacher too. The Minoans have even depicted a lion hunt; and if there ever was such an occasion in Crete the animal is likely to have been imported specially for the royal favour, or disfavour. The second point is about the hunting of the bull. There is no need to imagine that the bull was imported. But the only unequivocal representation of this animal being trapped and hunted—as opposed to being played with in the bullring—is on the famous Vaphio Cups, and though the workmanship is undoubtedly Cretan, Vaphio is in the Peloponnese. Since however the wild bulls were there in Crete, and the demand for them in the bullring must have been insistent, it is surely legitimate to take these cups as showing a genuine Cretan scene. More of them later; it is enough to say at the moment that bull-capturing must have been a highly

Clay seal of waterfowl, from Knossos

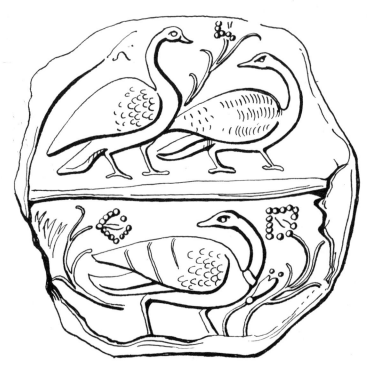

skilled and a highly dangerous occupation. In 1963 excavations east of Heraklion under the direction of Dr S. Alexiou, Ephor of Antiquities in Crete, brought to light an ivory box on which is carved a scene very similar to those shown on the Vaphio cups. The background is a natural one, not an arena; and supporting the acrobat doing the dangerous work are, this time, not men with nets but men with spears — perhaps they helped to guide the bull towards the nets.

There was little else of danger to hunt. The only other fierce animals were the wild cat, the badger, the weasel. The insect world gave the scorpion and a poisonous spider; of venomous snakes there was only, as in Britain, the viper. There are legends that Zeus, or alternatively Hercules, had cleared this fortunate island of noxious beats — a job not quite completely done.

What did the Minoan eat? Mostly barley bread, olives and goat's cheese no doubt, like most other people in the Aegean world. Crete exported olives, and the Cretan, unless the best were kept for export, must have done well with his olives. There is some evidence, rather slender perhaps, that his bread was not so good: a skeleton with his teeth badly worn down. Gourds and peas and beans would have been easy vegetables to grow; and honey, the ancient world's universal sweetener, must have been plentiful. Writers in classical times have given Crete a reputation as a grower of fruit, such as the fig, and of herbs; and the discovery and cultivation of all these were likely to have been made early in Crete, as they were elsewhere in the Bronze Age world. Early too was the dis-

Domestic utensils and cooking appliances (after drawings by J. W. Graham): (1) bronze tripod, (2) bronze lamp, (3) clay lamp, (4) grill, (5) oven, (6) ladle, (7) funnel, (8) egg tray, (9) bronze cup, (10) pitcher

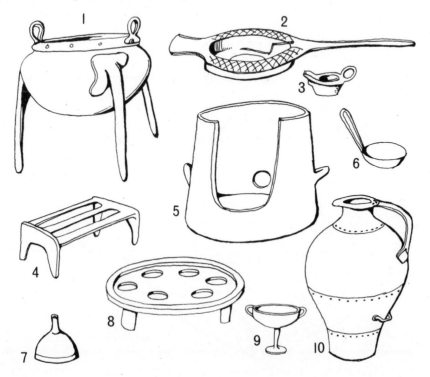

covery of the heart-gladdening properties of yeast—gladdening to the heart of man, that is—and of the possibilities of encouraging and controlling fermentation. The number and variety that has been found of both cooking appliances and containers of liquid and pourers thereof, seems to show that the Minoans were serious cooks and if not serious drinkers at least reasonably uninhibited ones. Nor have such discoveries been confined to the palaces. As has been said, sea food must have been plentiful, particularly the easily caught young squid. As for the flesh of beasts, the peasant at least is not likely often to have tasted it, though his superior may have done better. In the ancient world the killing of a beast was a special and solemn occasion warranting invariably—and it was so, right on into the times of classical Greece—a sacrifice to the gods. If the sacrifice was occasionally a good excuse for a meal of which the gods got little, the killing was still a special occasion.

The sailor in his ship was certainly carrying the olive, or its oil in great jars, as part of the exported wealth of Crete. And if the common man was the peasant, comprising 90 per cent of most Bronze Age people, then in Crete the other 10 per cent would have been made up largely of sailors together with the merchants who saw to it that the sailor got his cargo and the craftsmen who produced the more precious items of it.

One Cretan portrayal of a ship shows a horse on board; and as the artist has shown the horse about as big as the ship he was no doubt stressing the unusualness of the cargo—a point of significance which we will deal with later, the point being here that however unusual or unwieldy the cargo the Minoan sailor would cope. He was also well aware of the dangers of the sea, and in addition apparently did not deny himself the voyager's right to tell a good story. Another miniature Cretan seal shows a ship over the side of which seems to be clambering an enormous slavering monster.

Fragment of a seal-stone showing sea monster and ship

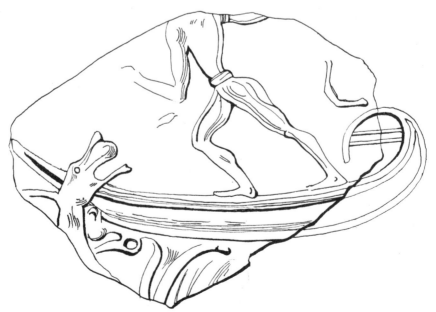

Cretan shipwrights must have learnt from Egypt and set the fashion in ships in the Mediterranean for centuries to come, the wily Odysseus's black ship included. Collated evidence gives this picture: a sea-going vessel, curiously high in the prow and low in the stern; carvel not clinker built; on average 70 feet long by 14 feet wide and as much as 100 feet long at the greatest; having at most fifteen oars on each side and one large square-rigged sail amidships; steered not by a rudder (which is an A.D. and not a B.C. invention) but by a long sweep. One piece of practical equipment, it has been suggested, may have been a cageful of land-homing pigeons, to be sent up, as a dove was once sent out of the Ark, when landfall was sought; it would be something to cheer a compass-less and monster-conscious crew. Cretan harbours were usually situated on each side of a promontory, so that approach could be made whichever way the wind blew. The long secluded roads of Suda Bay approaching modern Khania show no sign of Bronze Age use, such a narrow channel being perhaps feared as a too convenient hiding place for pirate ships. And in this connection, it does not have to be imagined that the Minoan kings, though they were, as the learned now put it, at the head of a *thalassocracy*, did as that word implies completely "rule the waves": piracy was too persistent and long established a Mediterranean occupation to have been wholly stamped out at any time, and the Minoans, a peace-loving people if ever there was one, are not likely to have possessed an invincible and militant "fleet" as did Collingwood's England or the Athens of Pericles.

This is not to say that the Minoan sailor's life was not hard or hazardous, but only that he was not likely to have been the member of a Minoan "navy". Even when putting down other nations' piracy he probably had professional soldiers on board, as was the sailor's usual practice almost up to Nelson's time; and there may have been times when

Minoan seal showing a ship

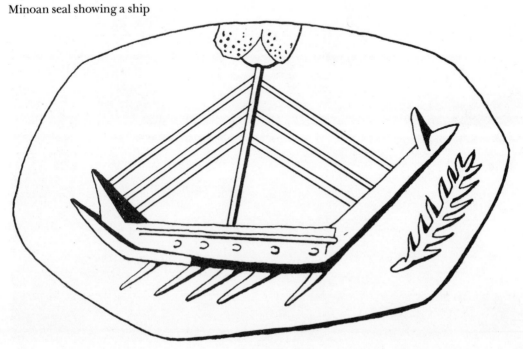

he was not above a little piracy himself. His voyages at times were no doubt adventurous and extensive. But more often they must have constituted an established and even monotonous run: from Crete to Egypt, up the coast to Palestine and Syria, across to Cyprus, and so via the islands of the Dodecanese home.

Even the giant jars, the *pithoi* (plate 4) that filled the ship's hold with oil and wine and raisins, were themselves works of art and in spite of their size graceful. But, as has been suggested, there was likely to be at times more precious cargo being carried abroad, and the craftsmen of Crete, working both for export and for the home aristocracy, must have made up an appreciable slice of the population.

Of the craftsman's products, as potter, as painter of pots, as bronze-smith, as fresco artist and as mason and architect in the building of great palaces, we shall have a deal to say later; here we are concerned with the Cretan's way of life. However, the extent, variety and beauty of the craftsman's products must mean that he was a highly respected and even often a highly placed member of society, and the vivacity of his work ought to

Giant *pithoi* at the north entrance to the palace of Mallia

mean that he was a happy worker. In the early days many an artist must have sailed to Egypt to learn his trade; and in the last days many an artist, having surpassed his tutors, must have sailed in the opposite direction to take on the task of embellishing the courts and palaces of the barbaric but forceful Mycenaeans. Meanwhile, in the palaces of the nobles and the houses of the rich, protected from the heat of the day and with the equivalent of the "north light" in the form of light filtered and reflected down the shaft of a "light well" (of which more later), he had his workshop—and left behind enough of his tools and materials of trade for the later archaeologist to be able to recognize many such workshops as he has unearthed them.

At Gournia, on the northern coast where the island is narrowest, have been found the tools of a more humble craftsman, a carpenter. This is how Harriet Boyd Hawes, who with her husband started the excavations there, describes the find:

> A whole carpenter's kit lay concealed in a cranny of a Gournia house, left behind in the owner's hurried flight when the town was attacked and burned. He used saws long and short, heavy chisels for stone and light for wood, awls, nails, files, and axes much battered by use; and, what is very important to note, they resemble in shape the tools of today so closely, that they furnish one of the strongest links between the first great civilization of Europe and our own.

There is another site, a beautiful one called Hagia Triada or Holy Trinity, there being there the remains not only of a Minoan palace but of a medieval chapel. Here were found—amidst very much else, as later will become evident—some saws of enormous size that would have been capable of dealing with the timber of the great cypress trees that still were plentiful, as also at least the softer stones, to produce as in Egypt the ashlar or squared masonry that before the coming of bronze was an impossibility. These must have been precious tools, as were indeed all bronze tools, for neither copper nor tin is a plentiful ore. The carpenter of Gournia was most careful of what may be called the tool that made his tools. With his cache of implements was discovered a block of schist, into the sides of which were cut moulds for the casting of chisels and awls and nails. Says Mrs Hawes:

> This stone was so precious a possession that when it cracked in a jagged line across the top, the owner used the utmost care in mending it. First he drew a narrow strip of copper twice round the block, binding this fast with turns of the strip, and then he drove in flat stones as wedges between the strip of metal and the block, a neat piece of work. . . .

So much for the artisans who together with the sailors and the peasants were the backbone of ancient Crete and helped to create her greatness. But what of the towns and villages in which they lived, the houses which our careful carpenter helped to furnish and to build? The palaces, as also the great ones who were masters of them, we will leave for later chapters and the more detailed description they deserve. Homer speaks with awe and admiration of Crete's "hundred cities"; and as he was writing about three quarters of a millennium after the Minoan heyday, the island's reputation must have been extremely powerful. For city we may of course read town or village; and it must be realized that such would be likely to include all classes of people, the farmer and farm-

The Town Mosaic, discovered at Knossos,
showing different types of houses

worker and serf included, the isolated farmstead being a modern phenomenon, the ancients preferring the protection and friendliness of each other and of their lord in his house on the hill.

It was at the beginning of the Middle Minoan Period that building seemed to receive a great impetus and that palaces and villas, with towns or villages round them, sprang up. Skill grew rapidly and some of the best building was done in the Middle Period, better often than in the Late. The main cities grew large by any standard, the estimate for the population of Knossos in the Late Period being 70,000 at least.

The cities do not give any great impression of being planned. Rather they grew outwards from the focus of power and prestige and protection of the royal palace or rich man's villa, a more natural thing to do. The general impression they would give to anyone approaching them would have been much as of a modern village or little town in Crete or Greece or on the Aegean islands, though sometimes on a larger scale: a close-packed huddle of white houses glistening in the sun, usually square in shape but as a whole not regimented, flat-roofed and often with an outside staircase to break the severity of line. On a series of panels that were discovered at Knossos set into the sides of a wooden chest, and called the Town Mosaic, house fronts are shown: the majority

Plate 1. Two views of the Cretan landscape, both in the neighbourhood of Phaistos and showing the Mount Ida range in the background. *Photos: H. E. L. Mellersh*

The ruins of the port of Gournia

of two stories though some are of more, and we can assume that two stories was the most likely size for the average "middle class" family house.

These mosaics of houses, it will be seen, show windows with panes; and the reasonable assumption is that oiled parchment filled the panes, as in Egypt—taken down perhaps during the long summer months. Excavations show that the houses usually stood flush with the street, facing inwards on to a central open patio, the more humble equivalent of the palaces' famous light-wells. In the patio the cooking was probably done, only the rains of spring and autumn driving the housewife within, there to use a portable clay hearth such as was even used in the palaces and to deal with the smoke or charcoal fumes as best she could. Six or eight rooms would have made a good average better-class house, but as many as twelve rooms was not unusual. Their furnishing would no doubt have seemed bare to modern eyes though not necessarily severe. Stone benches and platforms are shown in excavation; and it must be remembered that, unlike the Egyptian, the Minoan climate was not dry enough for the preservation of wood or leather or fabric. Nor is a civilization so gaily clothes-conscious as the Minoan seems to have been, likely to have scorned comfort or to have disliked brightness in the home. We may imagine rugs and cushions and hangings to alleviate the severity. Traces of a pale blue distemper have often been found on inner walls, the colour of the moulded ceiling of the queen's living room at the Knossos palace.

Many houses would of course be smaller than those shown on the Town Mosaic. But they would have been far from hovels. An imagined visit to Gournia may help us to

Plate 2. Where Ariadne may have danced: the "theatral area" and the steps leading down to it, at Phaistos. *Photo: H. E. L. Mellersh*

gain a fair impression, that town by the sea which eventually saw disaster and where the carpenter hid his tools. There the bared ruins do give an impression of cramped quarters. But then the foundations of a modern house always give a false impression of smallness. The impression to be taken from Gournia is, rather, a wider one. Here lies one of what may be called the first towns of Europe. And it is a town in its own right. Though the nobleman's or the rich man's villa may be there, it is only *primus inter pares*. This town, lying in its trough of the hills facing the sea, was a port and had its business as a port. Here, as was then mostly the custom, the traders' ships would be drawn up on to the friendly beach: perhaps because here is the narrowest part of the island, they were sometimes carried overland right across to the south shore, thus causing remunerative work for the locals. Two further aspects of Gournia are significant. It had no fortifications—it was open to the sea from which it drew its wealth. It had an open space, a market place, an *agora*. Greek cities, it will be remembered, were always to have an agora, and to use it as a place of meeting and discussion as well as of buying and selling. The Cretans are not likely, from their self-portraits, to have been a glum or silent people, so perhaps they started the fashion that eventually turned the agora into a forum.

At all events, and whatever the legacy that they bequeathed, we may legitimately imagine the towns of the Minoans to be pleasant and prosperous places and to be filled with largely happy and prosperous people. That is the impression that the later Greek legends gave; and there has been found nothing to disprove it. The town lies white and glistening in the sun—and if nowhere does the sun shine always, in Crete it shines a great deal—and above it stands, as guardian but not tyrant, the palace with its colonnade of bright painted pillars and its flying pennant. The pillars are archaeologically verifiable, and, since the Egyptians taught the Minoans more than a little and the Egyptians invented this fluttering symbol, the pennant is a justifiable invention . . .

Chapter Four

THE PALACES

Labyrinthos meant to the Cretan "The House of the Double Axe" — and if there was that pennant flying from the palace's highest point then at Knossos at least the double-headed axe would have been its symbol. But to the Greeks a labyrinth was something different, a large building with numerous and intricate passages, in fact a maze. It is an accepted idea, and a reasonable one, that the palaces of Crete gave the uncivilized but impressionable early Greeks this idea.

Knossos, Phaistos and Mallia are the greatest palaces of ancient Crete, and the Cretan legend is that they were once ruled over respectively by King Minos and his two brothers, Rhadamanthys and Sarpedon. Mallia lies on the northern coast some twenty miles east of Knossos, and Phaistos lies near to the southern coast thirty miles to the south-west. Roads connected both Mallia and Phaistos to Knossos, and the beginnings of them out of Knossos can be traced. The one to Phaistos and beyond to the coast must have been ancient Crete's main artery of trade. J. D. S. Pendlebury, who walked most of the ancient routes, said that this one could be covered in twelve hours, with an extra two hours to arrive at the sea. Skirting Mount Dicte as it does, however, it can by no means have been a level or an easy road.

More of these roads later. Of the three palaces, connected by their roads, Knossos was the greatest. No doubt in early times all three were the seats of petty kings; but the legend of Minos and his brothers suggests that by Middle Minoan times and the time of Cretan greatness the king of Knossos ruled the whole island. Nor should the word "labyrinth" and the legend of Theseus and Ariadne and the clue of thread give us the impression, whatever was the untutored Greeks' impression, that the palace at Knossos was a muddled and amorphous conglomeration of casually connected buildings. Knossos, and the other palaces too, did spread themselves over the ground, but it was an ordered and intentional spread, and there was also some imposing height to the buildings. Arthur Evans, excavator of Knossos, spoke of it proudly — proudly, because he was its re-creator — as "a crescendo of spacious corridors, peristyles and halls, served beyond by a stately staircase". Knossos is indeed the very epitome of the Cretan palaces; its name found its way into the *Iliad,* and for the later Aegean world Knossos must have been synonymous with ancient Crete. And since it was also the first site to be systematically excavated, we shall do well to accord it a detailed description.

First, something of its excavator or, as we have said, its re-creator. Arthur Evans, born in 1851, was the son of a well-known antiquary and a child of rich parents. He grew up to be an amateur numismatist and a professional newspaper correspondent whose particular interest and sympathy lay with the peoples of the Balkans in their struggle to shake off the dead hand of Turkish rule, a sympathy that occasionally showed itself in a

The "corridors, peristyles and halls" of the
palace of Knossos, from the queen's megaron

somewhat individualistic and high-handed way. Restless in his subsequent appointment
as Keeper of Oxford's Ashmolean Museum, Evans continued to pay visits to the Balkans
and to Greece, and when after only a dozen years of marriage and at the age of 42 he
lost his wife, the call of the lands of the Aegean grew stronger. That was in 1893. He had
already met the German discoverer of Troy, Heinrich Schliemann, and had visited his
excavations at Mycenae in the Peloponnese. Now in the Athens Museum Evans became
fascinated by the ancient and beautifully cut seal-stones which that institution possessed.
His short sight was a help rather than a hindrance in studying their minuteness, and he
was particularly interested in some of the seals that showed a hieroglyphic writing in an
unknown script which, he was told, came from Crete.

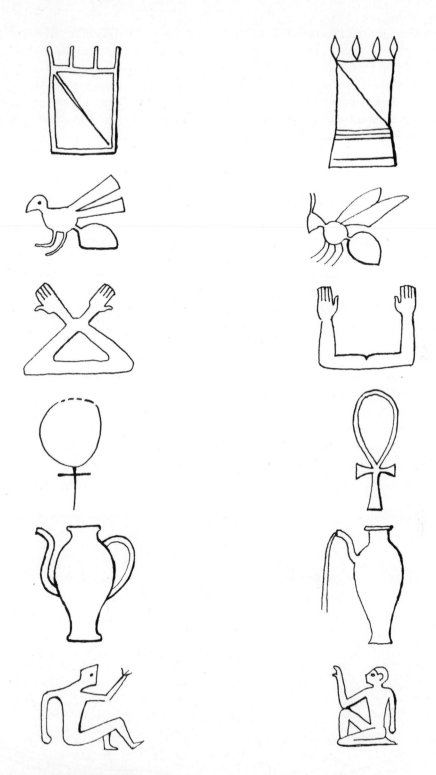

Examples of hieroglyphs from seals, showing
similarity of Minoan (left) to Egyptian

It was in the pattern of Evans's life that he should meet with difficulties from the Turks, to whose enemies he had given so much sympathetic support. It was also in the pattern that he should be attracted via Greece to Crete. Schliemann's discoveries had opened up great new vistas. The progenitors of the classical Greeks—then called Aegeans, now Mycenaeans—had before his discoveries been no more than a myth and legend, and by the historians discounted as such. Schliemann had made them real—and given more than a slight indication that they had been both powerful and important. But whence had they come, and in particular who were *their* progenitors in the spread of cultures and civilization? It was with that query that Evans took up the story. He had nothing to guide him but the legends, the allusive references of classical authors—and the seal-stones.

Evans was unfortunate in that he never succeeded in deciphering the hieroglyphic script that had first attracted his notice nor even the later scripts that he discovered. But he was at least fortunate in that he succeeded in obtaining permission to dig at Knossos where his famous predecessor, Schliemann, had failed—there may in fact have been something more than luck involved, for Evans, if as forceful, was a little more tactful than his German rival. It was a slow and difficult job nevertheless. In 1894 Evans had managed to purchase a quarter of the site of Knossos, which was known but virtually untouched; but revolution against Turkish rule broke out and it was not until the last year of the nineteenth century—with the Cretans happily free—that he could begin his great work.

The great thing to realize in considering Knossos is that Arthur Evans and his helpers had practically no idea of what or how much they would find. The seal-stones, of which Evans had managed to collect more in Crete, bore similarity to seal-stones discovered at Mycenae, some of which depicted men and women wearing a most un-Greek style of dress; they also gave evidence of a great and surprising artistic skill. Here however were no more than vague hints. To say that evidence of a brilliant new civilization was not

Mycenaean seal-stone from Thisbe

hoped for would be untrue, for hope springs eternal, and there was always Schliemann's spectacular success at Troy to be remembered. But what could not possibly have been imagined was that a civilization was going to be discovered so spectacularly unlike anything that had gone before. Something of the excitement and amazement of Evans and his team can therefore be understood as they unearthed this huge and novel architectural achievement of the Minoans at Knossos and as they unearthed its pottery and uncovered its frescoes. Some of the difficulties can also be imagined, first of excavation, for here were the remains of two palaces, one built upon the other and both upon earlier occupation, and secondly of interpretation. The two constituted a life-work for Arthur Evans, and he lived to be ninety; they earned him a knighthood and cost him a private fortune.

One point may perhaps conveniently be made here and before we proceed any further. It concerns the knowledge that we now possess of the Minoans. As is well known, the Minoan script — not the hieroglyphics that Evans studied with his myopic eye but its final derivative — was deciphered only recently (in 1952) by the late Michael Ventris. But, though a remarkable amount of information can be extracted from the decipherment, the only writing so far interpreted and translated was used on the mainland of

The restored west entrance to the palace of Knossos

Crete for, it is believed, no more than a short fifty years or so; and it was used only for pay rolls, inventories and the like. We are still dependent for our knowledge therefore chiefly on all the other, material, finds, together with what we feel we may interpret from the legends. The finds, however, proved to be extensive . . . .

Knossos may disappoint the modern visitor. But then most ruins will do that. Knossos is unusual in that Sir Arthur Evans, discovering very often masonry at different heights and levels, has gone to great pains not only to preserve all that is preservable but to support and augment it with concrete blocks and lintels and pillars. This does two things. It makes it much more possible to understand the original layout and to an extent to visualize it; but it also destroys much of the air of antiquity and constricts the imagination — no longer, one feels, would it be possible, as did the foreman set to watch over the first discovered frescoes, to have strange dreams. However, the Minoans of the Golden Age (MMIII and LMI and II to us — see Chapter Two) did not have to worry about the sight of door jambs of concrete painted over with varnish to represent the grain of wood; and it is fundamentally the Minoans and not the present-day remains of their palace with which we are concerned.

To the Minoans the palace must have been — between earthquakes — a marvel and a source of pride: to the king a home and a seat of power; to the court lady, whose image, in intimate miniature, we have recaptured from its walls, a place of intrigue and gaiety and, no doubt, occasional boredom; to those craftsmen who had their workshops there a place of work like any other; to the foreign slave a place of awe and foreboding; to the acrobat of the bullring, a place of excitement and terror. Its very approach was magnificent, across a great bridge or viaduct that spanned a shallow valley and a stream. We may people that as we will. But surely it must at times have been crowded and busy, for like most palaces of its time in this and other civilizations it was a large and self-contained entity, a combination of medieval country estate or Roman villa and — to use not wholly parallel modern images — Whitehall, the Houses of Parliament, Westminster Abbey, the Docks, the Tower of London and the Mint.* Crossing the bridge therefore might be seen not only the well-dressed palace people but the exotically dressed — exotic to the Minoan — merchant recently arrived at the nearby busy quayside; the diplomat; the suppliant; the favoured tradesman or peasant with his wares and produce; the shepherd with his flock of sheep for the royal slaughterhouse. Equally often perhaps the long bridge would be quite empty, for we must not people the ancient world with modern-sized populations; and in the Mediterranean world there is the siesta. Then only the sun would beat down, and a single cicada flit across the bridge, a hesitant lizard run along its balustrade, and time move on unobserved.

One thing however might well have surprised the stranger, whether he came to disturb this peaceful scene or to be involved with the herd of sheep. Here was a bridge but no draw-bridge; and in front of him he saw no high defensive walls.

The palace of Knossos can be reduced to a plan. At the centre is a great open court-yard, about 20,000 square feet in area — the whole palace covers about six acres — and on one side of it, the west, are the official apartments and on the other the private. There

---

* Bronze ingots, in the inevitable shape of the double axe, were found at one of the palaces, but not of course coins.

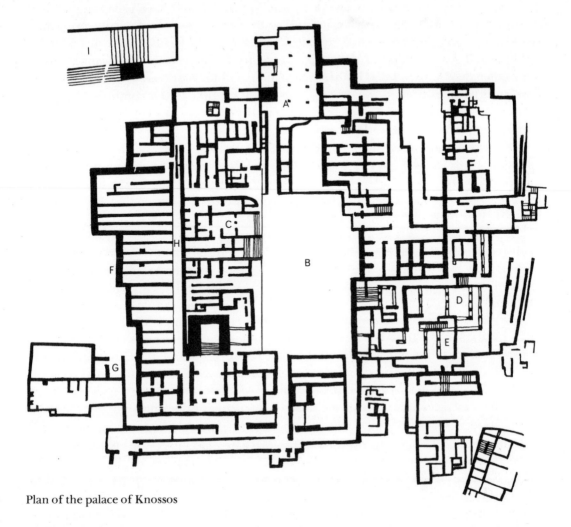

Plan of the palace of Knossos

A North Entrance
B Great Courtyard
C Throne-room
D Hall of the Double Axe
E Queen's megaron
F West Court
G South-west portico
H Corridor of the magazines
I Theatral area

will be more to be said about the official side in later chapters, for under this heading comes also the religious; but one or two features bear on the Minoans' general and private ways of life and may be noticed here.

Had you entered the palace your rank and business would have governed your route. A peasant or merchant would have come to the West Court, equivalent of the tradesman's entrance. Here he would have waited until his business could be attended to. Then his produce, whether for sale or by way of taxes, would have been weighed and measured and stored. All along, facing this court, were long rows of narrow magazines (plate 4), opening inwards on to a connecting alleyway, which, since there was no light-well here and great halls stood above them, must have been very dark. The great pithoi, some taller than a man, stood in these magazines, and for more treasured articles there were covered safes let into the ground. One pleasant note to this commercial activity: it has been noted that the wall of the West Court had along its shady side a stone seat for the convenience of the waiting customers.

The more important visitor, and the superior members of the household, would approach from the north-west, in fact along the final stretch of the great road from the south of the island, after it had crossed the viaduct. They might have stopped for a meal or a night's lodging at the hostel or caravanserai across the river, where a bath for their tired feet would have been brought and where they could have admired the frieze of partridges and hoopoes as they dined. At this north-west entrance, under shady trees, one may still enter the palace precincts and still tread visible remains of this "oldest road in Europe" (plate 5). First architectural feature to be met with is the "theatral area", a paved open space, flanked on two sides by shallow rising steps, and of which an even more impressive example is to be found at the brother palace of Phaistos (plate 2). Room exists for a considerable audience on the steps, and there is a place for a dais for the king. A fresco of a girl dancing, her long locks flying, has been discovered; and the placing of the dancing floor here may indicate a custom of welcoming back the king with dance, or of dances to finish off a solemn procession. Homer tells of a "dancing place that in wide Knossos Daedalus wrought for Ariadne of the lovely tresses": perhaps here is the very place and perhaps the fresco is a portrait of the king's daughter herself; at least, those who like to think so cannot very well be gainsaid. . . .

Having passed through a propylon or entrance gate, the courtier or high-born visitor would then turn right and leave behind on his left the quarters of the artisans and clerks. Now he would be challenged by sentries—for if Knossos conspicuously lacked fortifications there is evidence that reasonable care was exercised at this important northern gate—and would pass up a narrow inclined ramp between solid masonry, to find himself in a pillared forecourt. Here he would be faced with the startling and life-like fresco of the head of a charging bull—and he would know for certain if he had not done so sooner that he had indeed arrived at the capital of the Minoans. This sloping ramp still exists and above it has been rebuilt the pillared portico and the fresco of the bull restored (see page 15).

Passing on, duly impressed, the visitor would reach the great open central courtyard of the palace, the focal point about which the whole vast structure must have been built. On his left and to the east the buildings would stand low, for a reason to be explained shortly. But to his right the façade of the west wing would stand three stories high.

Reconstruction of this façade has been possible, and Piet de Jong, one-time curator at Knossos, has painted a picture of the impressive sight that must have faced the visitor. Pillars of a most distinctive kind would have been in evidence, rounded pillars and made of wood painted russet colour and with black or bright blue painted pediments. These pillars of Knossos were also, it has been discovered, wider at their top than at their

The theatral area at Knossos

base, a curious shape that nobody can now explain; one suggestion is that originally the pillars had been no more nor less than lopped and uprooted trees and that to use them upside-down would have prevented them sprouting!

In this western façade the greatest of the pillars support an open entrance and stairway, and up this stairway our visitor might well have marched, to be ushered into some great reception hall on the floor above. What in fact filled this floor it is now impossible to say with certainty; but Evans, taking an analogy from the *piano nobile* or "principle floor" of Italian medieval palaces—which contained the great reception halls and were never on the ground floor—has imagined the same plan for Knossos: no one can make a better suggestion, and "piano nobile" this now non-existent floor has somewhat inappropriately remained. On either side of the staircase the visitor would not be likely to penetrate, for to the right, facing him, lay the throne-room which is likely to have had a deep religious significance as well as a kingly; and on his left were other religious chambers behind a pillared shrine. Such a pillared shrine is depicted in the miniature "Temple" fresco, of the crowds of spectators and the gossiping girls (to be noticed in greater detail in the following chapter). It has led one commentator to believe that spectacles, the bull-game included, were held in the central courtyard itself.

There we will leave our hypothetical stranger. For the throne-room and the pillared shrine have significances more proper to later chapters, and no one will ever be able to reconstruct the halls of the *piano nobile*. The private quarters or the eastern side of the palace provide a more intimate human interest, and also show the greater architectural

45

skill. In order to utilize to the full a situation open to favourable winds and the morning sun but sheltered in other directions and remote from the hubbub of the West Court and the public business of the North Entrance, the Minoan architects actually cut away part of the slope of the steeper side of the low hill on which the palace stands and formed a partly artificial terrace twenty-five feet below the level of the Central Court. They then built *up* to the courtyard.

The chief feature of the east or private side is the famous Grand Stairway (plate 6). Down this the king, leaving behind the cares of father of his people, or of priest and supplicant of his god, having crossed the Great Courtyard, could descend to his queen and his family and his private life. The great staircase is not wide by Versailles or English country house standards; but it is a major architectural feat, it is imposing and it would be wide enough for the king to be preceded or followed, and perhaps more so than he wished, by great panoply and pomp of officials and courtiers. Four flights down brought him to the Upper Hall of the Colonnades and five to the Lower Hall, the columns running up through the floor and both rooms being lit as usual by the mild reflected light of a light-shaft. (The colour plate shows how effective these light-shafts could be in a climate of intense sunshine; the principle is often used in modern office blocks, but in spite of glazed bricks not so effectively.) If the king turned left he could reach the Hall of the Double Axe, but if right he would reach, be devious passages, the Queen's Hall or Megaron.

All these names of rooms are of course modern, given because of what was found there, or as a good guess at their use. They are by no means vast halls; rather they are royal apartments that could have been comfortable and even intimate. The familiar sign of the *Labyrinthos* was found often incised into the masonry of the Hall of the Double Axe. But in this room has now been hung, in the belief that they have merely replaced originals, replicas of great figure-of-eight shields. These appear engraved on a

Figure-of-eight shield, from a Mycenaean sword

Mycenaean sword and furnish yet another link between the Minoans and the nearby warriors of Homer's *Iliad*. Such a shield was nearly the height of a man, was covered with double ox-hide, and must have been rather more than Odysseus, or any average Minoan, could conveniently have lifted, and might even have caused Achilles a little trouble. Hung on a wall, however, they are magnificent.

The Queen's Megaron, as re-created by Evans's artists (plate 9), is a room of delightful beauty and colour and grace. Here was found the fresco of the lowest of the three dancing girls shown in the reproduction and part of the dolphin fresco, also enough fragments of ceiling to establish its pattern. The feature of the room, long and narrow, was its division into two, each part having its own light-well and the dividing pillars being surrounded by a stone bench.

The king, making his way down the dark dog-leg corridor to his wife and relaxation, would have passed the queen's bathroom and lavatory. Here we are brought conveniently to that less romantic aspect of Minoan skill which nevertheless always arouses the greatest interest on the part of visitors to the site of Knossos, that of drainage.

The bathroom, about seven feet by twelve, must have been pleasant enough, with its wooden beam and pillar (thought to have been fluted on analogy from that in another washing place) its gypsum* floor and ornamental dado; but it must have been dark, lighted only over a balustrade dividing it from the megaron. For this reason the reproduction by Evans's artists has been made to show a lamp, a pedestal lamp of lotus shape such as was found in remains in many parts of the palace. Remains of the terracotta bath were found just outside the room; it dates somewhat later than the room itself and may have been, as it were, a modern refinement in the last days of the palace. Even with this however, since its bottom measurement is only just a metre (39^1/$_3$″), bathing could not have been a matter of comfortable wallowing but of having water poured over one by obliging slaves.

As to the even smaller room, its discoverer writes as follows:

> On the face of a gypsum slab to the right is a groove for a seat about 57 cm. from the floor. Outside the doorway of the latrine is a flag sloped towards a semicircular hole, forming a sink, and from this opens a small duct leading to a main drain. The aperture leading to the main drain, partly masked by a curious projection, deviates from the centre of the seat, thus leaving room on the right for some vessel used for flushing the basin. As an anticipation of scientific methods of sanitation, the system of which we have here the record has been attained by few nations at the present day.

Perhaps Sir Arthur Evans was a little hard on his "present day". Writing of the drainage system more generally, he describes how the underground drains, which also took the water from the roofs in the rainy season, were ventilated by air shafts and made accessible by man-holes "so roomy that my Cretan workmen spent whole days in them without inconvenience". The sections of terracotta pipe, he adds, fitted neatly into each other and were made slightly tapering so that they "were admirably designed to impart a shooting motion to the flow of water so as to prevent the accumulation of sediment".

---

* Gypsum is a whitish crystalline stone, not so hard as limestone, used extensively at Knossos. It is a hydrous calcium sulphate.

The autumn rains could be heavy, and on the steps down to the East Bastion a particularly neat bit of architectural engineering was discovered. A channel had been cut at the side of each flight of steps to take away the excess water. But these flights, quite steep, were at right angles to each other and the problem facing the Minoan architect was to slow down the flow of channelled water so that at the right-angle bends it would not spread out over the landings. They solved the problem by constructing the fall of the water channels in a series of *natural* curves, the curve being the parabola. This device about halved the rate at which the water reached the platform. "Nothing in the whole building", says Evans, "gives such an impression of the result of long generations of intelligent experience on the part of the Minoan engineers as the parabolic curve of the channels." Perhaps it may be added that the fresco of a fountain suggests that the Minoans did not encourage their engineers to be purely utilitarian.

To describe the palaces of Mallia and Phaistos as repetitions of Knossos would be to do them an injustice. But they are on much the same plan and include in their layout the same dominant features. Mallia covers an area nearly as large as Knossos, and Phaistos is about two thirds of Knossos in size. Neither, incidentally, was excavated by Evans; the first was tackled by French archaeologists soon after Evans had begun his work at Knossos, and the site of Phaistos is still being excavated by the Italians.

Phaistos is on a commanding site and Mallia on a lovely one. Mallia overlooks a bay so peacefully idyllic, with its bright sand and its clear rippling water, that it provides a perfect opportunity to call to mind one other legend that, like Plato's Atlantis, both describes a happy land and gives hints that the author had Crete in mind.

It is the story of a princess who was not too proud to do her own washing, and it is related in Homer's *Odyssey* and takes place in the mythical island of Phaeacia. Bright-eyed Athene, ever thoughtful of the welfare of her protégé, Odysseus (who has been washed up on the island and is sleeping exhausted), arranges the happy episode. She puts it into the head of Nausicaa, the king's daughter, that she shall go with her maidens to the shore and the mouth of the little stream, there to do her washing. Her mother, in modern language, makes her up a picnic. She is most thoughtful for the welfare of her daughter, and includes not only a goatskin of wine but "a golden flask of olive oil, so that she and her maids could anoint themselves after bathing".

It is while they are playing ball on the beach after their bathe that the awakened Odysseus discovers them. He is welcomed modestly but kindly, fed with the remains of the picnic, and invited to make his way with the girls to the king's palace and the city. "Our city", says Nausicaa proudly, "has an excellent harbour on each side and is approached by a narrow causeway, where the curved ships are drawn up to the road and each has his separate ship. . . . It is here too that the sailors attend to the rigging of the black ships, to their cables and their sails, and the smoothing of their oars. For the Phaeacians have no use for the bow and quiver but spend their energy on masts and oars and on the graceful craft they love to sail across the foam-flecked sea." Arrived before the king, Odysseus is entertained in a quite splendid manner and is promised a safe passage home. However distant is his home across the sea, declares the king, his sailors will take Odysseus there. "Nor does it matter if the spot is even more remote than Euboea, which is said to be at the world's end by those of our sailors who saw it, that time they took red-haired Rhadamanthys to visit Tityos, the son of Earth."

Left. Fountain fresco in the House of Frescoes, to the north-west of the palace of Knossos

Below. The central court and altar at Mallia

This Phaeacia is of course a beautiful cloud-cuckoo land where all is gaiety and graciousness and the worst that can happen is a tiff over the games. But it does not need alone the reference to Rhadamanthys to make the scholars believe that memories of ancient Crete inspired the fairy tale. Stand on the beach below Mallia, and it needs no effort of the imagination to see Princess Nausicaa and her maidens playing there at ball.

In speaking of Phaistos we may quote one more passage from the *Odyssey* before dismissing its slender but fascinating evidence. "So forward now," commands the King of Phaeacia at one point in the elaborate entertainment of Odysseus, "so forward now, my champion dancers, and show us your steps, so that when he gets home our guest may be able to tell his friends how far we leave all other folk behind in seamanship, in speed of foot, in dancing and in song." An outstanding piece of excavation at Phaistos is the dancing floor or, as the archaeologists have called it a little more prosaically, the "theatral area" (plate 2). It is larger than its counterpart at Knossos and gives more obviously the impression of being a place for dance or shows. The Knossos floor has shallow steps leading away from one side of it and these might be taken at first sight as being no more nor less than steps. But those at Phaistos rise straight up to a solid wall. The assumption must be that they are steps for sitting or standing, and not for walking.

If Daedalus built Ariadne a dancing floor it might well have been at Phaistos and not at Knossos. This is pure speculation, of course. But another speculation, perhaps less idle, that must I think occur to anyone walking the courtyards of Phaistos, is that Ariadne would most certainly have delighted to visit this place. "Ariadne" is believed to mean "the Holy One", and whether Ariadne was one single person or the title of the king's daughter, whoever that king might be, just as Minos is thought by some to be a generic title—whether in fact there were many Ariadnes or one, they or she would surely have been drawn to Phaistos as a place to uplift the spirit. The palace stands on the brow of one of a row of steep hills rising from the broad valley, and beyond that valley to the north runs in the distance the great blue range of mountains with Ida herself dominating all. And just below one of Ida's twin peaks can be seen sometimes a little dark round hole which they say is the entrance to the cave where legend has it that Zeus was born. It is not too fanciful to imagine Ariadne's eyes being drawn to that holy spot—though it is beyond our imagination to guess what would be her thoughts. It certainly has the effect of an all-seeing eye.

Phaistos has an offshoot of a smaller palace at the site called Hagia Triada, already mentioned. This smaller palace has been christened the summer residence of the ruler at Phaistos, though with no greater reason than that it seems a likely possibility. What is a fact is that considerable relics of a religious nature have been found there, of which more later. Here again is a possible attraction for the "holy" king's daughter. What is also a fact now, and must have been a fact then, is that the view from the "summer palace" at Hagia Triada is superb. It surveys a gulf of the sea which is now called by a name that fits it, Hagia Galene or Holy Tranquillity.

Phaistos has been subjected to none of the elaborate restoration that Arthur Evans bestowed on Knossos and for that reason it is less easy to understand the layout of the ruins. But these ruins—of limestone whereas Knossos is mostly gypsum—lie in the sun as pale golden as a Cotswold village, and they are very beautiful and very evocative. Just

Plate 3. Ivory figure of a bull-leaper from Knossos, sixteenth century B.C.
Photo: Holle Verlag

The palace of Hagia Triada and the Bay of Hagia Galene

as in the season grapes are heaped upon the visitor here, so in one of the great *pithoi* at Phaistos was found a like intimation of bountiful and well-tended harvests — grape seeds still lying at the bottom of the jar. It is impossible to believe at Phaistos and Hagia Triada that before calamity came by earthquake or invasion the Minoans were living other than prosperous, happy and gracious lives.

Plate 4. One of the giant *pithoi* or storage jars at the palace of Knossos.
Photo: Picturepoint

Chapter Five

THE PEOPLE IN THE PALACES

It is possible to dig up a people's past and still have very little idea of what they looked like. We cannot recreate an image of the palaeolithic cave artist because he shied away from making a lifelike picture of himself. Outside Homer's descriptions we do not know the Trojan, unless the grinning faces on jugs are portraits, equivalent of the Winston Churchill toby jug, which is unlikely. In the same way Arthur Evans, even after he had been digging for some time, had virtually no idea of the appearance of these people he was both discovering and naming. There were admittedly the seal-stones. But what human figures these showed were mostly Mycenaean and in any case were often not likely to be human in the strictest sense but, rather, divine, and no one can tell how meticulously or otherwise a particular man has created a particular god in his own image.

The day therefore when Evans discovered at Knossos the fresco now known as that of the Cup Bearer (plate 7) was an outstanding one. There was revealed the image of a young man vital and handsome, thoroughly un-Greek in dress and appearance, and indeed altogether surprising.

What, perhaps, on taking thought, should be surprising, is not the Minoan costume but

Keftiu, from Egyptian monument

the classical Greek costume, for it is easier to imagine the evolution of the Minoan than the Greek. But rather naturally the discoverers saw the matter the other way round: they expected the Minoans, "the first Europeans", the forerunners and teachers of the Greeks, to look at least something like their successors and pupils. They did not. They looked highly distinctive. If anything, and to employ an Irishism, this cup-bearer looked like a remarkably un-Egyptian Egyptian. The ever-boastful pharaohs of Egypt's New Kingdom were fond of showing foreigners bearing tribute, and among these they on occasion showed people described as islanders and called the Keftiu. There can hardly be any doubt at all that the Keftiu were the Cretans. The figures carry vases and jugs that look Minoan; and though the Egyptian artist cannot wholly get away from his traditional way of depicting the Egyptian smooth-cut hair he does show the Keftiu to have long hair and even allows himself a restrained effect of curliness. More significantly he shows the short kilt, folded over and coming to something of a point between the legs. The real point, however, is that this kilt is not unlike the Egyptian kilt. Both are a natural evolution from wrapping a skin round one's middle.

Another magnificent fresco, also uncovered at Knossos, is that generally known as the Priest King, where a young man in a plumed head-dress leads something which is out of the picture and is imagined to have been a sacrificial or symbolic beast.* This and the Cup Bearer together give a very good idea of Minoan costume – as worn, that is to say, by male Minoans of the upper sort. With the Priest King the kilt has become a kind of sheath with cut-away drawers, a form of garment also usually shown as worn by the bull-leapers, probably made of leather and padded for comfort, and in the case of the bull-leapers, for protection. For the rest, and except for the ceremonial head-dress, there is similarity between the two figures. Whatever the way of dress owes to Egypt or to obvious evolution, these figures have three very distinctive characteristics: the long curling or stranded hair; the great use of jewellery, bracelets, arm-band and collar; and the con-stricted waist.

The general effect is not foppish as our long-haired but over-dressed Caroline cavaliers were foppish, at least not so in these two figures, which are noble and vital. Nevertheless, and to say the least, the effect is striking and shows a high consciousness of male beauty. The way of wearing the hair the Mycenaean warriors seem to have copied – Homer calls them the long-haired Achaeans – so that it was a fashion that could certainly go with manliness. The same may be said of the wearing of jewellery: heroic and romantic but not effeminate. The Cup Bearer's bracelet looks remarkably like a modern identity disc, and possibly it was; in any case it is perhaps relevant that in the two world wars of our own generation it has been the habit of men to substitute for the dull official edition of such a necessary adjunct to a dangerous life a more delicate affair of silver: thus is danger to be faced, and the male duty to face it, romanticized. And if this does not much tally with the idea of the Minoan as a peace-loving and unmilitary person, we can remind ourselves – as we shall in more detail later – of the dangers of the bullring.

* Frescoes are usually shown as now reconstructed, the original parts made slightly darker to be distinguish-able. It may seem sometimes that the reconstructing artist has taken much liberty and not a tight enough hold of his imagination. But closer study will show that he has always had something to guide him, either in parts of the picture being reconstructed or in other similar pictures. It may be, though, that we shall for ever know the Minoans a little tinged by the imagination of Evans's gifted Swiss artist, Monsieur Gilliéron.

The Priest King fresco (restored) from Knossos

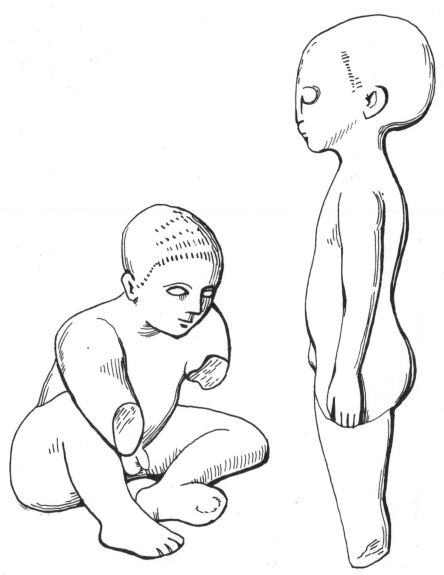

Ivory figures of young boys, from Palaikastro
(after a drawing in Evans: *Palace of Minos*)

The fashion of artificially constricting the waist seems to come under the same category, not effete but romantic. For if the true-bred Minoan was naturally broad-shouldered and narrow-waisted, and if he was proud of his appearance, then it was a fairly natural thing for him to accentuate the characteristic. That the fashion was taken to such extremes, however—always making allowance for exaggeration on the part of the Minoan artists—is surprising and must be significant. Sir Arthur Evans made what he believed was an important discovery here. It seems obvious from many frescoes and figures that the Minoan male belt was a metal one. Now such a constricting belt is not shown on ivory figures of very young boys, while it is shown on the figure of a boy who

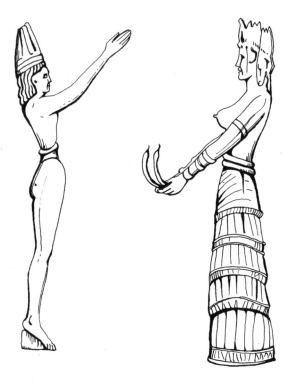

Group of belted "boy god" adoring snake goddess (after a restored drawing by Gilliéron in Evans: *Palace of Minos*)

Bronze figure of a worshipper, loosely belted; found at Tylissos

looks, he says, about ten years old. Further, allowing for the possibility that it was fitted a little loose, the belt of this figure gives the expected proportion to height and shoulders as shown in figures of grown men. The metal belt therefore may have been fitted at the age of about ten. (It ought to be added that this particular figure of a boy, one of those known as a "boy god", was not actually found by Evans in Crete but turned up in Paris: some people have questioned its authenticity, though not the master himself.) Evans makes a further point on the same subject, which is hardly open to question. "It does seem, however," he says, "that as a concession to the broadness and obesity often inherent in later years, the wearer might eventually be relieved, a less tightly fitting belt, probably of leather, substituted." As evidence he cites a relatively portly figure found at Tylissos, and also the sistrum player on the Harvester Cup. It will be seen incidentally that the rest of the peasants in this scene do follow the fashion of restricting the waist, though they do not let their hair fall to their shoulders as do the aristocracy, either cutting it short or more probably rolling it up on the top of their heads as the Homeric heroes rolled theirs beneath their helmets.

The custom of restricting the waist therefore appears to be a universal one. What is also apparent is that it cannot possibly have had any detrimental effects on physical suppleness or freedom. The wearing of the belt must have gone with a great regard for slim fitness and a dislike of obesity, and so of gluttony. This is in some contrast with

The Ladies in Blue fresco

Egypt and the East, where the well-fed priest is an often depicted figure; but it is in line with the later Greeks, who made a virtue of lean living. Even the Minoan elderly figure is by no means obese. We may, however, perhaps imagine him having visited the bronze-smith for relief, as we visit the dentist or the chiropodist. Then, on coming away, none the worse for his long restriction, he would no doubt boast on all possible future occasions of a youthful measurement of, say, 38 – 18 – 22, the middle figure being verifiable by the broken but carefully preserved metal waistband.

The ladies of ancient Crete — except for the girl bull-leapers who in all respects appear dressed as the men — are also portrayed with slender waists, perhaps if anything more slender. In all other respects their dress is totally different. It is elaborate where the male, except for the wearing of jewellery, is simple, and it is to anyone still thinking in terms of classical Greek costume even more surprising.

Before considering the female Minoan costume it will be as well to realize what are the sources from which our knowledge is gained. In the maze of lower rooms in the north part of the Knossos palace were found, fallen and in fragments, frescoes that when put together again were rightly called "miniature", for though they showed scenes that were large and crowded their total width was only a few feet and their human figures seldom measured more than a couple of inches. This fact is quoted not to cast doubt on all interpretations based on the frescoes, for the amount of revealing detail etched in by the

Three details of the Temple Fresco

Minoan artists is phenomenal. But it should perhaps act as a restraining influence on any too soaring flights of fancy. That Arthur Evans somewhat indulged himself in this way—one lady "raises her hand in amazement, 'You don't say so!'" and another does the same "in depreciation of her sharp-tongued neighbour"—we may surely forgive. But we others have less right to go so far, and certainly not farther.

Nevertheless, that much having been said, let us look at these female figures without seeking to curb at least our astonishment. The seated ladies across the centre of what is known as the Temple Fresco, together with those of the Ladies in Blue Fresco, are

Plate 5. Sometimes called "the oldest road in Europe": part of a paved way on the outskirts of the palace of Knossos. *Photo: Picturepoint*

Overleaf. Plate 6. The staircase of the palace of Knossos, as reconstructed by Sir Arthur Evans. (Stairs at bottom left, pillars of the higher landing at top centre.) *Photo: Holle Verlag*

the best examples. Nothing else that is of the second millennium B.C. has been discovered that is at all like them. The stiff hieratical figures of Egypt, the dumpy, inanely smiling effigies of Sumeria, the embodiments of male, monarchical ferocity that have come out of the Indus valley or early Assyria, have no connection whatever with these gay Minoan figures. Even the bronze dancer from the Indus valley, if graceful, is quite impersonal. The Egyptians liked to portray happy human scenes on their walls. But these are pious delineations of a hoped-for bliss in a future world and the portrayal is downright and seemly: there is no suggestion of the conversation piece, no glint of humour, no hint of caricature.

These Minoan ladies *are* gay, *are* sprightly and vivacious, whatever exact interpretation we choose to give to their expressive gestures. With their elaborate and jewelled hair-dressings, their long gaily coloured skirts with bands of flouncing, their puffed sleeves and provocative, breast-baring zouave jackets, they are obviously highly sophisticated, fashionable creatures; they justify the description, "court ladies", and the Frenchman's sobriquet of "Parisiennes". From the way in which they are shown as obviously indulging in chit-chat among themselves, while the crowd are more properly intent upon watching whatever spectacle they have come to watch, it is obvious that they are intended to be shown as pampered and sophisticated ladies; that they are given prominence in the picture shows that they are important people.

These facts give rise naturally to the question, is the dress of these gossiping girls therefore exceptional? They seem to be seated in some sort of balcony and between them and on each side of them are what look like the pillars and platforms of some sort of sanctuary or temple — hence the title of the fresco — while all about them is a huge crowd. The crowd is portrayed by a sort of conventional shorthand: heads only are shown and in swathes of terracotta or white, the first being men and the second women. And what do we see? Not only are the standing figures about the pillars dressed similarly to the balcony ladies but the female heads in the crowd seem as gay and curled and decorated as theirs. No doubt everybody for this occasion, whatever it was, is dressed up to the nines; no doubt the court ladies set the fashion and live up to it if not beyond it. No doubt too, as ever, the peasant workaday costume was simple and freer, and the more elderly in all walks of life, in this sex as in the other, were exempted from the more exacting dictates of fashion. But for the rest, and when all is said, this strange, provocative, flouncy costume does seem in essence to be the normal one. Whether the breasts were bare or covered by a diaphanous chemise, as a frequently shown line about the neck seems to suggest, remains a disputed question; though in either case the coquettishness, or as we should think — or used to think? — the immodesty, remains. Whatever it revealed, the costume was an elaborate one, and as a whole it presupposes a tremendous amount of sewing and embroidery, as it does also of tailoring and fitting: as somebody has said, it is not a sculptor's ideal of dress but rather a corsetière's.

It is a costume likely to have arrived at the fashionable from the religious. Priests in ancient days may often have shaved their heads, as a symbol of cleanliness perhaps, and have danced naked. But the religious propensity is usually in the other direction, a plethora of clothes, since clothes create a new and different person and also give great opportunity for both dignity and symbolism. The priest therefore often wears a skirt — the Sumerian does; the Minoan himself does, as is shown on the Hagia Triada sarcophagus; even, as somebody else has pointed out, the modern clergyman does. And as for the priestess, she does the same, and perhaps even more so. We have as evidence for ancient Crete, the effigies of the "Snake Goddess". More will be said of these later. But here at least it may be stated that this "goddess" is just as likely to be a priestess, and that her skirt is elaborate indeed. There is also the imprint from the gold signet ring from Isopata (plate 14), near Knossos. Here the goddess is the small figure above the wavy line, a line used traditionally to divide heaven from earth, and the major figures below are therefore certainly priestesses. And they show the same elaborate dresses, with the flounces mostly sweeping down to points in the front of the dress, as are shown on the standing figures in the Temple Fresco. There are the same bared breasts — which, where a Mother Goddess or her priestess is concerned, are no doubt appropriately symbolic of fecundity, fruitfulness and fertility.

One cannot imagine much symbolism about the gossiping coquettes of the Temple Fresco, or "La Parisienne" (plate 8) though she does wear a "sacral knot" at the back of her neck, or even the dancing girl. What, then, has happened? Knowing that the nemesis of destruction awaits Knossos, one turns inevitably to the explanation of decadence. But that may be too hasty a jump. For Arthur Evans produces good evidence that the miniature frescoes do not date from the last years of the Minoan golden age but from the end of the Middle Period, in which case there are some hundred and fifty years to run before catastrophe. Nor is secularization necessarily a sign of decadence; perhaps rather it is only the sign of a healthy capacity to extract enjoyment out of the least likely material and an ability not to take religion always too seriously. Our Edwardians did something of the sort when they managed to make the dress of a quakeress a vehicle for musical comedy glamour. And even the Egyptian ladies turned the long linen priestly skirt into a diaphanous affair, and the Egyptians were extremely religious.

Perhaps we are seeking a rational explanation where none is possible, and seeking to

Left. Faience snake goddess

Right. Painting of Sir Arthur Evans's reconstruction of the Hall of the Double Axe at Knossos

66

understand the Bronze Age mind when we should do better to acknowledge that it is too far away from us ever to be understood. A magnificent ambivalence may have been possible, indeed must have been possible. The Minoans were, by all the signs, unobsessed by religion, certainly by any gloomy religion; they were sophisticatedly gay. Yet they were religious, as we shall see. Ariadne was by all accounts the holy priestess. Yet there stood at Knossos the queen's megaron; and she must have visited it and sometimes lived in it; and it was a supremely gay and cheerful and unportentous room.

Now that we have seen how the inhabitants of the palace dressed we can the better people it with them in our imagination. The reproduction by Evans's artists of the queen's megaron we have already seen. It will be realized now that there have been transplanted a couple of girls from the miniature frescoes and that they are as it were continuing their chat—though they will no doubt cease their chattering when the queen comes in, lest like Victoria she be not amused. It is a reasonable transplantation.

There is also the re-creation of a scene in the Hall of the Double Axe, a winter scene this time and depicting comfort rather than gaiety, but relaxation nevertheless. "This has been artistically executed," wrote Arthur Evans, "in accordance with my suggestions, and reproduces the effect of its splendid equipment of great body-shields suspended on the wall, as in the Megaron of Odysseus. Here the Minoan lord is seen seated at ease on his stool in a very different fashion from that imposed by the fixed canopy in the 'Audience Chamber'. He warms himself before a movable hearth, like those that have been found in a fragmentary state elsewhere in the Palace. . . . The doors and windows of the partition on the left, through which access was gained to the Western section of the Hall, with its Portico open to the light-court on that side, are shown mostly closed to keep out the draught, but, apart from the openings, the light filters into the dark corner of the Hall through the red-stained parchment panes."

Chapter Six

THE RULE OF THE DOUBLE AXE

The *Labrys* or Double Axe is the ubiquitous symbol of the Minoans. It became the symbol of the Mycenaeans and something like it even found its way on to Stonehenge, to confound but delight the British archaeologists and to demonstrate the universality of the Bronze Age civilization. The *Labrys* was in Crete more than a ubiquitous symbol, however, it was a royal one; or rather perhaps it was commonly used because it was royally used, a sign no doubt that imparted a feeling of importance, or of well being, or of luck or of borrowed power, to the user of it and viewer of it, as the cross was to become to the Christian and the swastika to many a tribe of pagans.

It is undoubtedly wrong to think of the axe as in any way a symbol of cruelly exercised tyranny, of bloodthirstiness. The axe is not typically a weapon, it is a tool. It is essentially the tool of the neolithic people who were the first farmers. Two tools they needed, the hoe which was the forerunner of the plough, and, more primarily essential, the axe to clear the bush and the forest so that they might use the hoe and plough. Their first tools were flint, which in use became polished; and the neolithic people then learnt to polish the stones before use, so that the polished stone, and the polished axe in particular, has become as it were their trade-mark to the present-day archaeologist, and rightly so. The axe could hardly escape becoming a symbol of potency to the neolithic peoples; and when bronze arrived the potency was merely increased, while the need to use the axe for its primary agricultural purpose remained.

It is true that the axe also became a battle-axe. But, as the sword has become a symbol of justice, so even the battle-axe can have an at least non-belligerent association as a symbol. No doubt a great deal could be learnt of royalty from the symbols they used. The mace is hard to soften into anything but a bloodthirsty, and bludgeoning, symbolism. The whetstone, which was the royal insignia in the Saxon cenotaph of Sutton Hoo, could be thought of as sharpening either the sword or the scythe; the crook and flail of the pharaoh neatly symbolises the beneficent ruler of an agricultural people, leader of the flock and at the same time thresher of the grain. What then does the double axe symbolise? Surely power and potency. It is not a bloodthirsty symbol, but neither has it the practical friendliness and helpfulness of the Egyptian symbols. Incidentally, what advantage a double-headed axe has over a single-headed axe is hard to see; one would imagine none whatever in real life, the duplication being no more than symbolic: a double-headed axe is twice as powerful, much as a double-headed eagle is twice as ferocious.

When we come to enquire what was the power of the dynasty of Minos and how it was administered we find our evidence admittedly rather flimsy. Let us make what we can of it—though not more than we should. The trouble is that the Minoans not only seem

Gold double axe from the cave of Arkalochori

to have had little history — until towards the end, that is to say — but also singularly to have had little sense of history. Perhaps the two go together: happy is the country which has no history; and happiness and political awareness — which is, we might say, historical awareness in the present tense — do not easily go together. Nor do the rulers themselves seem to have shown historical awareness, or the desire to make future generations historically aware of themselves, which is the next best thing and a very human desire at that. The Egyptian rulers were the very opposite in this respect, as were the Persians after them:

> My name is Ozymandias, king of kings:
> Look on my works, ye Mighty, and despair!

But in Crete there are no royal edicts, no royal monuments, no royal effigies – so far as we know, no delineation of individual "top people" at all. We can at the least draw a conclusion from this lack which as students we must deplore. The rulers of the Minoan people were, by comparison with most of their contemporaries and successors, a remarkably modest lot.

Perhaps we may draw an even further conclusion. Most boasters are not very certain of themselves; they "protest too much" – Ozymandias, alias Rameses II, protested all over the Egyptian landscape. By implication, then, the Minoan rulers were self-assured.

They are obviously likely to have been efficient, successful and beneficent, for there is the evidence of the prosperity and magnificence that has been dug up, and the evidence of the legends and universal reputation left behind of a "blessed isle". Where the rulers stood, however, in the gamut from fatherliness through bureaucracy to tyranny, is harder to say, though more interesting. Before we cite what material evidence exists to answer that question, there are two observations worth making. One concerns the fabled bronze giant, Talos, two of whose activities we omitted to mention. Whereas he sometimes strode the sea and hurled firebrands at enemy or piratical ships, when striding the land he was wont to display peaceably the brazen tablets of the law, for all Cretan people to see. The other concerns those same laws, the making of which is one of the brightest facets of King Minos's reputation. Laws are of little use unless there are efficient sanctions to enforce them. And here we come back to what was said in Chapter Two about the Bronze Age outlook. The sanction that a Bronze Age person needed and respected, as also the neolithic person before him, was a religious or supernatural sanction, the sanction of custom and taboo backed up by the disapproval of the gods – a disapproval no doubt made actively apparent by authoritative human hands, but nonetheless basically divine. So Moses went up into the mountain, the Sumerian king is shown receiving the tablets of the law from the god, and in Crete a supernatural figure displays those same tablets. If an ancient people were peaceably united, were homogeneous and had a common tradition behind them, if they were not plagued by the disturbances of wars and invasions – if they were fortunate in all this, then no heavy hand would be needed to enforce the law. Sanctions would be as effective as they were un-material, and punishments would be, though no doubt crude, seldom needed in practice. All the evidence goes to show that the Minoans existed in this happy state.

That the Minoan government was wholly undemocratic we may of course assume without question. That it was heavily paternalistic, and feudal, is highly probable. One discovery at Knossos, in a Middle Minoan deposit below the north-west corner of the central court, shows, and at an early date, something of a paternal or at least a centrally efficient government, concerned with the important matter of foreign relations or trade. This discovery is of a diorite statue of an Egyptian, actually giving his name, probably "User". "This monument", says Pendlebury,* "is exceptional in that it is the only

---

* in *Archaeology of Crete*, 1939, page 143.

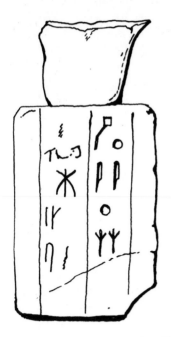

Back and side views of a diorite statue of an
Egyptian, from Knossos

Egyptian object found in the Aegean which must have a personal connection. Vases can be the result of trade, scarabs may be souvenirs, but a personal non-utilitarian monument such as this can only imply the presence of the man himself. It may be that User was the Egyptian ambassador to the court of Minos or that he was the agent of some temple sent to buy wood. . . . In either case the statue was no doubt dedicated in one of the Palace shrines, for wherever he went the Egyptian courteously paid his attention to the local god." Incidentally the fact that the Egyptian was undoubtedly of the early part of the 12th Dynasty proved a useful piece of Minoan comparative dating.

A likely evidence of feudalism in ancient Crete is the growth of rich country villas. This much may be said of Bronze Age Cretan history, of which we know so little and of which there may be so little to tell. After a long and prosperous neolithic age and with the Bronze Age established, there came, about 1900 B.C., a great outburst of building. The Minoans became thorough town-builders, and also palace-builders. This is the era of what is known as that of the old palaces. Then came, about 1700, a great devastation by earthquake. The people possessed sufficient vitality, and government was sufficiently established and resilient, for there to occur a century later a great recovery and a fresh upsurge of building. And now it was not only a rebuilding of palaces that occurred but also a building of large houses as well as of small. The country villa arrives; and often it is fine enough to be considered a minor palace, and important enough to attract the building of a small town around it. Often such villa and town were near the coast, seeking the benefit of foreign trade, the town still happy to receive as sole protection the mere presence of the villa.

"Lord" here is surely the appropriate word. The villa-owner may have been also a rich merchant; but the ancient world's aristocrat did not have the Victorian's scorn of trade, perhaps partly because trade was an adventurous and often dangerous occupation, and whether one sailed in one's own ships or not there was a glamour about it not unfitting to be associated with aristocracy. The site of Gournia, already mentioned, possesses such villas; others have been found at Palaikastro, at the eastern tip of the island, at Tylissos about ten miles west of Knossos, and at Nirou Khani, about ten miles east. More recently, in 1958, Professor Dora Levi excavated a large Late Minoan farmhouse at Gortyna in the Messara Plain. With alabaster-lined state rooms, frescoed halls, well furnished kitchens and well stocked storage cellars, they often amount to small palaces. Here must have lived the aristocracy that helped rule the country, the feudal chiefs, the local barons and "nomarchs" such as helped rule the Old Kingdom of Egypt, the difference being that there is no trace in Crete of their having revolted and taken power into their own hands as they did in Egypt to create the chaos of her euphemistically named "First Intermediate" Period.

The villa at Nirou Khani was so stocked with religious objects, including no less than forty tripod altars, that the supposition is that it was the home of a high priest, a sort of Cretan Lambeth Palace. Yet perhaps that is a misleading analogy, since religion is not so segregated in the ancient world. If Ariadne was the holy one and the king's daughter, then the high priest is likely to have been near to the king. In other words, here at Nirou Khani is further evidence that the villas were the homes of the aristocrats who were

Villas at Tylissos

ruling the land. An alternative, and ingenious, interpretation of this great store of ritual objects, made by R. W. Hutchinson, is that this villa, situated as it was beside a minor port, was "the Headquarters for the Propagation of the Minoan Gospel to the infidels in other parts of the Levant", the Mycenaeans, for instance. What that "Gospel" was we shall try to discern later. Whatever it was, or whatever was the cause of this phenomenal collection of cult objects, we may be sure not so much that there was a Minoan equivalent of trade following the Bible but rather that priestly paraphernalia need not be divorced from administrative paraphernalia and that whether the owner of this villa was the equivalent of a missionary or a bishop he was likely also to have been a king's satrap, a deputy ruler. There is in fact no sign of the Minoans living in an egalitarian society—and much sign of the reverse—and if the "coolie lines" of the workers' houses in the contemporary Indus valley civilization are an indication of what a Bronze Age egalitarian society was like, then the Minoans were fortunate that they did not live in one.

As H. G. Wells has pointed out in his *Outline of History*—others have no doubt done so, but he did it very succinctly—the man who wished to rule widely, to be a king of kings as the current international phraseology went, had need to look to his communications. And that is to use the word in its widest sense, material communications and unmaterial, physical and also psychical—roads and writing. The two go together. The man who can write down an order to a subordinate in another place, and can have that order conveyed to him, has done a very potent, indeed a magic, thing. He has enlarged his personality and his power, his aegis has spread. Writing and roads have created a new, and for him an infinitely improved, situation.

The Minoans had roads and writing. But both were a long way from perfect.

The model of a wagon was discovered at Palaikastro, and of a litter or sedan chair at Knossos—pictures and models are often the archaeologist's sole evidence, and he can only hope that the artist has been accurate and thank his luck that representationalism

Model of a wagon, discovered at Palaikastro

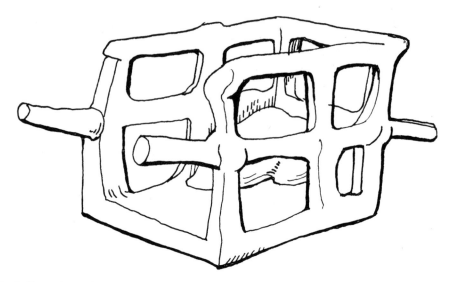

Model of a litter, from the Dove Shrine at Knossos

in art became taboo only in his own time. The model of the wagon dates from about 1900 B.C. and is a fairly primitive affair, as were probably all wagons at that date. A model of similar type but dated a little earlier has been found in Syria, and since Crete was probably already trading with the famous and ancient port of Byblos we may have here an example of the Minoans learning rather than teaching while engaged in their overseas adventures. In all conscience, however, it does not represent a very difficult lesson learnt. The wheels are solid and must presumably have turned with the axle, and there is no provision at all for the front axle to pivot. The ox would draw it, as the ox would draw the plough — and in Crete still does draw the plough — and one can only see this as no more than a farmer's wagon, used on his own farm.

The litter is obviously a humanly carried litter and may incidentally be regarded as another piece of evidence of a non-egalitarian society. Both these models suggest, in a negative and positive way respectively, that the roads of Minoan Crete were mostly mere paths over the hills and at the best narrow stone causeways, and that the traffic on them was not wheeled traffic at all. The road that enters Knossos is in fact a raised stone causeway only a few feet across. There would exist therefore no more than the palanquin for the highborn man or the fashionable lady, or for the king's messenger; and for the carrying of goods, the pack animal. The pack animal would be either human, carrying his load on poles balanced on his shoulder, or else the patient ass, with bulging panniers that drooped over the low parapets of the few bridges that crossed Crete's few and unnavigable rivers. If this seems surprisingly primitive for such a rich and sophisticated civilization as the Minoan we have only to remind ourselves that such were essentially the roads and methods of transport of most countries of Europe between the time of the Romans and the end of the eighteenth century. The long wide road was a necessity only for the far-flung empires kept down by the arms, and the marching feet, of soldiers. Driver of the pack-train must have been a common profession for the Minoan; and for much of the year, though not all, as he made his

The Phaistos Disc, side A

way under the sun, through the scented valleys, or the rustling olive groves, or between the ranks of cedar trees, it must have been a pleasant one.

The story of the evolution of writing in Crete is a complicated story, and the discovery of what use the Minoans mainly made of their writing is a somewhat surprising one, as well as disappointing. Equally complicated, and even more surprising in its result, is the story of the efforts to decipher the scripts: that story is outside the scope of this book however, and we must do little more than refer to it in passing.

Something of it, nevertheless. Things seemed to begin so well. Evans, after noticing hieroglyphics on the seal-stones, was rewarded early with discovery of clay tablets at Knossos, preserved by the lucky chance—lucky to him—of conflagration. Soon afterwards

The Phaistos Disc, side B

was discovered at Phaistos a thick clay disc, sixteen centimetres or nearly six and a half inches in diameter and covered on both sides with highly distinctive pictorial writing. The early promise however was not fulfilled. Evans, though he spent much time in sorting out the different types of script, in publishing descriptions of them (and incidentally involving the Oxford University Press in large expense in type-setting), never got much further than deciphering the Minoan numerals. As for the Phaistos disc, it proved not only indecipherable but also something of a red herring: most people now believe that it is an importation from Syria or Asia Minor; if some innocent merchant or sailor originally brought it home as a curio he would be amazed to learn of the trouble he had caused.

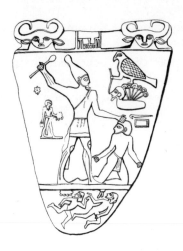

The Egyptian Palette of Narmer

The Phaistos disc at least shows a Minoan academic interest in writing and perhaps a sort of catholicity of taste. For it was discovered lying beside a tablet of what is undoubtedly Minoan writing, and it may yet be proved another variant of the island's efforts towards literacy. If so, the Minoans certainly took over some remarkably un-Minoan signs, for example what looks like a house on stilts or piles (which could be Lycian) and a lady dressed not in the least like the "Parisienne".

The principles on which writing has evolved, as also the fact that those principles appear with remarkable consistency in the evolution of almost all writings, are probably well known. A rapid resumé may however be justified.

The beginning is pure picturing. If you wish to talk about a horse, then you draw a horse; two horses, then two horses; five horses, then perhaps a horse with five strokes beside it. If a man, then you draw a man. If he is going on a journey, then you show him doing it, or—using a sort of shorthand, whereby the "pictogram" becomes an "ideogram"—you show beside the man a pair of legs, which means not "legs" but "walk". If you wish to portray a particular man, then beside him you will draw his characteristics or as it were his title, as on the famous Egyptian palette of Narmer, where the unfortunate man who seems about to be bludgeoned is shown to be none other than lord of the lower lands where lakes and fish abound—as it were Lord Fishpool—he having a fish-spear and pool portrayed beside him. Then comes the second step. If you can portray Lord Fishpool, then you can—to take a highly fictitious and English example—also portray, say, Lord Attlee, by drawing a *hat*—the lack of an aspirate here and there is of no significance—and a ley or meadow. You have in fact used the pun or rebus. You can extend the method: draw an ass and a pick, and you have (in English) aspic, very difficult to portray otherwise. You can now show not only names and verbs, but any other part of speech, so long as it, or its syllables, pun with a thing or things that can be drawn and recognized— "ram-page" for instance, to take a ridiculous example. You have taken the one necessary step, turning pictures of things or ideas into pictures of sounds. Having established the principle, you can even stretch it a little, so long as any particular convention is recognized by both writer and reader. Your only other need is to show by a "determinative" whether your picture represents a real thing or an idea or a sound.

77

So have the early writings developed, Egyptian hieroglyphics and Babylonian cuneiform included and Cretan writing not excepted. The great drawback is of course that pictures take long to draw, and the inevitable consequence is that the pictures grow increasingly simplified and stylized, more so in fact in cuneiform, which was executed with a wedge-shaped stylus on clay, and less so in Egyptian hieroglyphics which were painted with brush and ink on paper. The Minoan scripts in this respect follow rather the Egyptian hieroglyphics than the cuneiform.

Nevertheless the Minoan writing does become increasingly stylized, as also more competent and elaborate; and it was this evolution that Arthur Evans traced, distinguishing two types of hieroglyphic and two types of "linear" writing.*

It is the two linear types, called "A" and "B", that are important, the hieroglyphics being obviously pretty primitive and not greatly used. Of all the types only Linear B has been deciphered.

We come now to the surprising discovery, which did not so much throw a spanner into the archaeological works as turn the whole box of tricks upside down and give it a good shaking. It also makes the task of assessing the effects that the possession of the art of writing had upon the lives of the Minoans more difficult. It has to be faced however.

The late Michael Ventris was the decipherer of Linear B. He had his helpers, notably John Chadwick of Cambridge University; he had also his predecessors, some at least of whom helped him too. But the triumph was his. Results would have come more quickly if Ventris had not fought against the conclusion that was being forced upon him and which he and his contemporaries found not so much surprising as hardly credible.

Ventris had very little to go on in his task. There was no equivalent of a Rosetta Stone showing Linear B paralleled by a known writing. There was not the faintest knowledge of the Minoan language. There were only such tenuous clues as that names of places, such as Knossos, might be expected to appear and re-appear, that a recurring short collection of signs might well mean "and", that varying ends to words, to show gender, case and number of nouns or person and tense of verbs, might be expected. Ventris's work was, and had to be, infinitely painstaking.

Those word endings, the inflexions, proved themselves remarkably similar to Greek. More than that, the Greek language seemed to fit, and Greek names seemed to appear. In fact, that was the great surprise: Linear B *was* written in a variation of archaic Greek. Few experts now refute this finding. It had in fact been made more likely (once the unbelievable was accepted) by the discovery of tablets in almost exactly similar Linear B script at the Mycenaean palace of Pylos in the Peloponnese and at Mycenae itself. In fact, more Linear B has been discovered in Greece than in Crete, Knossos being so far the only Cretan site producing this writing. The date for its use in Knossos seems to be confined to the limits of about 1450 to 1400 B.C. Knossos at least, therefore, or rather the court of Knossos at least, must have been during that period Greek-speaking.

The wider implications of that discovery—together with the disputes that are raging as to what should be considered its correct implications—will be considered later. Let us now return to the central fact that the Minoans did possess a method of writing and consider what effect that possession is likely to have had on their way of living. There

*"Linear" not because written along a straight line but because made with a few stylized strokes as opposed to a picture.

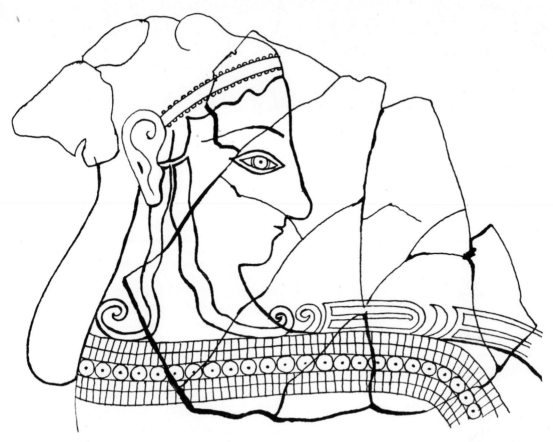

"Mycenaeans learnt from Minoans": part of a
fresco found at Tiryns, thirteenth century B.C.

does remain a difficulty, or rather a temptation to be avoided. We must be chary of accepting evidence of Minoan ways of life from the Pylos or Mycenae Linear B tablets, which are not only in the majority but are the more revealing. Mycenaeans learnt from Minoans, taking at the very least their way of dress from them; Minoans towards the end must certainly have learnt from Mycenaeans; but the two peoples, we must always remember, were very different peoples.

However the following facts remain, annulling to some extent the significance of the Greek intrusion. The writing was wholly a Minoan invention, owing general inspiration no doubt both to the Middle East and to Egypt. Linear B is no more than an extension of Linear A, having many signs the same. The use of one type of script does not neatly follow in time the use of another on the island: Linear B appears nowhere else than at Knossos, Linear A seems to be an invention and speciality of the Phaistos area, whereas Mallia seems to have had a predilection for the old-fashioned hieroglyphics, perhaps using them in a consciously archaic manner as the Babylonians used Sumerian cuneiform for religious texts and as we sometimes affect medieval lettering.

The other significant fact about the scripts is a sad one. Linear B—and presumably the

Figures on a Linear A tablet, which resemble Linear B figures

other scripts even more so—is not a very efficient form of writing. It is a second best, a cumbersome, hit-or-miss sort of writing. Many middle consonants are missed out, as are a final *s, n,* and *r* and the *i* in diphthongs. This means that short words can be read in as many as fifteen different ways. Partly no doubt for this reason, and for others which we can only guess at, the use of the writing was highly restricted. No equivalent of the Epic of Gilgamesh or the Story of the Flood has been found or is ever likely to be found, no royal edicts or even boastful royal declarations of prowess, no praises of the gods or incantations or even magic curses. The use of this writing, this half-cock, inexpressive, limping, creaking script, was confined to what, with the help of some quite adequate arithmetical signs, it was in reality solely capable of: inventories, receipts, accounts. It is the tool never of the poet or the historian, always of the bureaucrat.

The bureaucrat was a feudal bureaucrat, and even these accounting documents are often very human ones. They are the office records of that seat-of-government plus country-estate which we gave as description of the Minoan palace; they speak often in terms of workmen and slaves, of flocks and teams of oxen for the plough, of cows by name, and of the issue of cloaks and tunics. Of course there is also reference to stores and commodities, from bronze tripods and cauldrons to wheat and barley and olives. Here was the wealth of a kingdom in a world that had not yet invented money; and the kings of that time were, from all the evidence, highly conscious and proud of that wealth. That the Minoans and Mycenaeans should have developed such an elaborate efficiency in keeping count of it is nevertheless surprising: in calling their mode of government a feudal bureaucracy we should, it seems, put the accent much more on the second word than we should ever have believed likely.

Let us look at a few of the Knossos tablets and their translations, to see what knowledge we can gain of this Minoan "economy" which called them into existence and which deserves, so much more than we should have thought probable, such a high-sounding title.

80   Plate 8. The fresco from the palace of Knossos known as La Parisienne. *Photo: Hirmer Verlag*

Overleaf. Plate 9. The queen's megaron at Knossos. The reconstruction is the work of Sir Arthur Evans's artists and is reproduced from his *Palace of Minos*

The entries usually show the name of the person concerned and a sign to indicate whether it is an issue to him or a tribute from him. If it is a tribute the name of the town or village so taxed may be shown. Then will come the item concerned, the number thereof received or issued, together perhaps with some short comment, such as "so many short". The item is always shown in pictogram and not in phonetic writing, and it is interesting to see how these pictograms vary in the extent to which they have become stylized and simplified. The numbering is significant. The system was a decimal one, that is to say, the natural one based on the number of a man's fingers and thumbs, and the one that the Greeks and Romans adopted. The Minoans were however in one respect in advance of their followers. They did not invent the use of the zero sign nor separate signs for the numbers 1 to 9. But they did use *position*. That is to say, although, in the usual elementary fashion, they repeated a sign the requisite number of times to designate a number, for instance four short vertical strokes for 4, yet they had a different position for digits, tens, hundreds, and so on, and put each kind progressively to the left. As an example, the number one thousand, two hundred and thirty-four was -◇-°°- ̄ ‖. On that system one can add and subtract on paper — which is more than one can do with Greek or Roman numerals. As for fractions, no less than twelve signs have been recognized though it is not known what all of them signify. A *half* and a *quarter* are shown by a pot-hook right way up and upside down respectively and *three-quarters* by a combination of the two — which of course it is.

One word of warning. The examples from the Knossos tablets that follow are taken from Ventris's and Chadwick's *Documents in Mycenaean Greek* (Cambridge University Press, 1956), and rather naturally the extensive notes and comments and provisos that those experts have added to their entries have not been included. All that can be said here is that the translations vary in their certainty.

First, people. Here is something that indeed stretches the word "accounts", pretty widely. But land ownership and number of workers concern a central administration as much as stores; and among the Knossos tablets, found scattered over practically the whole palace and obviously representing only a tithe of what once existed, are those that show evidence of what might be called both a Domesday Book and a Census. The signs are:

Man   Woman

Perhaps the woman is wearing a long dress.
Here are two typical entries:

At Lasunthos: two nurses, one girl, one boy.
At — — —to: nine female slaves of A-no-zo;
one *da* —, one *ta*; two older women under
instruction; seven older girls, ten younger
girls, two older boys, two younger boys.

Da and *ta* seem to be abbreviations; of what, we are never likely to know.

Plate 10. Pottery of exuberance and grace. *Top* Late pots of naturalistic flower design.   85
Centre "Kamares" or Middle Minoan pottery. *Bottom* Early style, likely perhaps to
remind the modern reader of a toucan. *Photo: Hirmer Verlag*

Here are entries of workers, "on the strength" as a modern quartermaster would say:

> At Pharai: wages for 18 men and 8 boys:
> grain per month 1,170 litres of barley.
> Total men of Amnisos: nine; the
> rations are to be from there.

Amnisos was the port of Knossos. As to the first entry, it is interesting to note that if you treat men and boys alike, and give thirty days to a month, the ration works out at one and a half litres (or just over two and a half pints) a day—at any rate, more than sufficient in the way of carbohydrates. (Of course in arriving at litres the translators have had to make calculations that are open to amendment. The smallest Minoan measurement is a cupful—and comparison with other known ancient standards gives an idea of the probable size of the cup.)

Not many of the Knossos tablets refer to men by profession or trade, though this has proved much more common at Pylos. There is reference to a carpenter, however; and also this, from the Knossos palace muster-roll:

> . . . .two followers on account of tribute; Ki-
> ta-ne-to at Su-ri-mo on account of dues. . . .priest
> at E-ra, shepherd on account of dues; Kopreus,
> follower, of Exos.

Ki-ta-ne-to is a proper name—or rather a syllabic approximation to a proper name. The title "follower" is significant, and one often recurring at Pylos. It is likely to mean, either in the religious or the military field, an aide or assistant, probably a more important person than the word signifies to us. The longest Knossos tablet lists sixty-seven men by name. A few are Greek-sounding names; a short selection of the others read: pa-me-si-jo, mi-ja-ra-ro, si-ja-pu-ro, pi-ja-si-ro, pi-ja-se-me. These rather read as if—as among the Carthaginians of a thousand years later, where every other person seemed to be called Hannibal or Hasdrubal—there were not many combinations of name to go round: perhaps like the Welsh of today the Minoans talked of Jones the Baker. On an analogy with place names, those ending with *o* would be pronounced *os*.

Now livestock. Here are some of the signs:

Ox or bull	Cow	Sheep	Goat	Pig	Ass	Horse	Deer

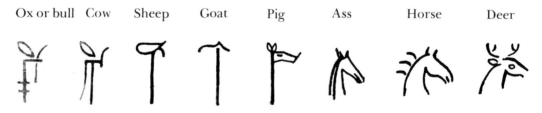

It is tempting to suggest that those outlines the least stylized are likely to be of those signs the least used and so of animals the most scarce, and *vice versa;* this would give sheep and goats as the commonest and horse and deer the rarest—which is more or less as expected. It is perhaps strange that there are not separate signs for ox and bull, for the difference would certainly be a significant one to Minoans. The entries begin with a man's name, presumably the shepherd's, and sometimes also show that of the "collector", i.e. tax-collector. The totals usually add up to multiples of ten and presumably represent a tax allocation, not always reached.

They are sometimes quite large; in fact the grand total of rams from one series of tablets comes to the surprising figure of 25,051. Here are a couple of typical entries:

> Rams 202, ewes 750, he-goats 125, she-goats 240, boars 21, sows 60, bulls 2, cows 10
> At Kudonia: 50 working oxen.

The comparative numbers are significant; as is also the fact that Kudonia was in the west of the island, the less populated part, but coming nevertheless under the jurisdiction of Knossos.

One set of tablets actually gives the names of yolk-pairs of oxen: Mr Chadwick has translated them "roughly" as Darkie (Xouthos) and Dapple, Winey and Whitefoot, Blondie and Bawler. This is indeed a human touch. One cannot imagine the actual rustic owners to have spoken in Greek, however, and this must surely be some meticulous scribe's effort at translation from the true Cretan names which we shall never know.

A simple tablet of horses and asses is here shown, and because it is shown we will quote it in a little more detail. It reads:

> First line: *I-quo* HORSE 5; HORSE 4 *po-ro*; FOAL [number broken off]
> Second line: *O-no* ASS 3 *po-ro*; FOAL 2; ASS 4.

Linear B tablet from the North Propylon at Knossos

The words in italics are syllabic writing, those in capitals are pictograms; numbers are vertical strokes. The final translation, taking into account both the writing and the fact that the pictograms show small but important differences (e.g. the very last shows two nicks on the neck, a usual sign for masculinity) is:

> Horses: five mares, four (full grown) horses, *x* foals.
> Asses: three she-asses, two foals, four he-asses.

This tablet, discovered by Evans at the north entrance passage, beneath where now stand the pillars of the Propylon and the head of the charging bull, is one of the few Knossos tablets that speaks of horses. It is not one that would have greatly taxed the intelligence of the scribe-accountant whose stylus pricked it out thirty-four centuries ago. The careful drawing of the animal heads would take him some time.

Signs for staple food products were:

Wheat   Barley   Olive oil   Figs   Spices

Spices fill an important part of the picture—and if we call them "condiments" the sign for them, which is exactly like a pepper pot, becomes highly intelligible. Knossos mentions cyperus and coriander seed. and Pylos adds sesame and cumin and fennel and a few more which are unrecognizable. More significant are the references made to the land that produces the foods, vineyards for instance and plantations, and occasionally to the ownership of it. Knossos again, however, produces disappointingly little evidence compared with Pylos. There are possible references to a "fief" and to communally held or common land. Pylos gives a definitely feudal picture.

Cloth and clothing, house implements and furnishings, all feature in the inventories. The sign for cloth ☐ is presumably showing the loom weights, but the sign for wool is less intelligible; it is taken over from Linear A and may have become more stylized. Linen as well as woollen garments are listed and there is reference to dyes, including the ancient world's beloved purple. There are "clean-edged" and "dirty-edged" cloths, which may lead us to think of stream-side laundries, though not necessarily under the care of the king's daughter. There are cloaks "suitable for guest-gifts", and others "of better quality" for "followers": possibly the palace officials were entitled to a periodic issue of formal clothing, as they were at contemporary Ugarit on the Syrian coast.

As for household utensils, they are many and varied, and explicitly portrayed: containers for liquid of various sorts being the most common. The broken tablet from Knossos here shown makes one think of a Victorian bedroom, and perhaps not wrongly: Knossos and Windsor of a hundred years ago may at least have had in common an army of ewer-carrying menials. Two other entries are more in keeping with a richer and more romantic aspect of the palace: "Two bull's head rhytons gilded (?) on the horns" and "Three silver cups. . . .the rim of gold". These are fitting items for any Bronze Age

Linear B tablet showing household utensils

king's treasury, as for that matter are the bronze tripod-cauldrons referred to. There is of course no reference to iron, but there is to lead, used perhaps as substitute for tin as a necessary alloy with copper to make bronze.

So the uses of Minoan writing. Owing to its inadequacies, its inexactitudes except when resorting to pure pictograms, no more literate uses are likely ever to be discovered. Its existence presupposes not exactly an army but a goodly number of scribes. It also presupposes that rather sinister phenomenon for the young which must have been appearing more pronouncedly in other parts of the Mediterranean world, the priestly school. For the first time the intelligent boy—unhappily or happily for him as we choose to think—is segregated from his peers, and while they roam wild, or learn the manly sports, or at the worst recite the tribal lays, he is incarcerated and subjugated to endless copying of the hieroglyphs. We may be quite certain that the royalty and nobility and gentry of Minoan Crete did not learn to write, nor must we allow ourselves even a tinge of scorn for them in that they were "illiterate". It would not be worth their while to be anything else. As well expect a Russian or Austrian archduke of the nineteenth century to feel the need to acquire the skill of a bank clerk.

There are two other types of entry on the Knossos tablets, scarce but significant and also possibly significant in that they are scarce. One concerns chariots and horses. The other, offerings to the god. We shall return to them both.

Chapter Seven

THE ART OF THE PEOPLE

There is great talk among the *cognoscenti* about the "eidetic vision", meaning thereby the capacity of some people, particularly primitive people, so to retain a visual impression, as the least of us retain an impression of a looked-at scene upon the shut eyelids, that they can with ease transfer it later to paper or any other convenient surface. The palaeolithic cave artists must have possessed eidetic vision, say the pundits, but the neolithic artist did not, since he was more usually content with pattern rather than picture. But the Minoan Bronze Age artist possessed it again.

To suggest that the ladies of the blue fresco, or La Parisienne, might impress themselves upon the eyeballs of any Minoan, artist or otherwise, may not be considered intelligent criticism; but it is perhaps intelligent criticism to suggest that the eidetic principle is an altogether too facile explanation of great artistry. It is a theory worth quoting, however. Another explanation of the skilled and enthusiastic naturalism of the Minoan artist also connects him with his distant predecessor in the Stone Age caves. Given the tradition and convention that his unbridled activities are in fact allowed, the artist will delight to portray what he knows well and is in close contact with in his life. The palaeolithic artist painted the animals he hunted; the Minoan the creatures of the sea and the flowers of the field. He also painted in a totally uninhibited manner what the cave artist never dared to paint except in an almost unrecognizable formalism, his own human kind.

If that is so, we ought to inquire why there existed a convention and tradition that did allow this freedom. It is a freedom that the Greeks inherited, but not a freedom usual in the second millennium B.C. It is not easy however to give a satisfactory answer — except to say that such was the nature of the Minoans. What they have left us adds up to an inescapable impression of an uninhibited, uncomplicated, gay and simple people, not so greatly worried by religious obsession or taboos. If you are such a people you are likely to love, unaffectedly, the beautiful things that surround you in daily life.

We must not ourselves paint too rosy a picture. Minoans certainly had their religion and no prehistoric religion was without its darker side. That we will consider later, and such art as is strictly concerned with religion.

The frescoes we have regarded only as portrayals of Minoan appearance and dress. They have other aspects, however. The young prince, wearing his fleur-de-lys necklace, followed by his butterfly through the field of waving irises, "walks in beauty and of cloud-less climes". And these irises, it will be noted, give an air of naturalness though they are nevertheless formalized — so much for the simple eidetic theory! It is possible to paint any form of life correct in outline, correct physiologically, and yet for it to be dead. The point has been made about the Cat and Pheasant fresco from Hagia Triada, that "summer palace" that produced so much both of beauty and of religious significance. H.R. Hall, writing of this, says:

> The Minoan borrowed his idea from Egypt, and his cat is in one sense a better cat than the Egyptian, in another a worse one. It gives the idea of the cat, its stealthiness and its cruelty, better than the Egyptian paintings which hardly give such an idea at all. But they [the Egyptian] are more accurate.

The appropriateness or otherwise of the eidetic theory is not of importance. What is of import and significance is the consummate artistry of the Minoans. It is easy to gush about art, and it is most off-putting to read such gush: perhaps the less written about art the better. But the Minoans were great artists, and it would be ridiculous not to stress the point. Theirs is a sort of controlled *joie-de-vivre*, with the control, the technical efficiency, the art that conceals art, so efficient, that is to say doing its proper job so well, that the joy is indeed not confined. Let the reader pause, and look at the reproductions in this and other chapters; he must then agree, I think, that those who found these things were discovering something quite new in heights of artistic skill and sensitivity.

Something also that needs to be realized about the frescoes is well shown in the "Parisienne" fragment (plate 8). It has been carefully cleaned; and it shows that the Minoans were not afraid of bright colours. The queen's megaron, with the dancing girls, the dado of fishes and dolphins, the pale blue scrollwork of its ceiling, must have been, as we like to say, a riot of colour—and the Minoans, and also the Greeks after them

The Blue Monkey fresco from the House of Frescoes at Knossos

The fresco of the Saffron Gatherer; the figure
in this restored fresco is shown as a human
being, but it is now believed that it should be
a monkey

with their painted Parthenon, must have preferred an exuberant riot to any cold
austerity. The king's throne room may have been as colourful; but the decoration, which
probably dates from the last fifty years of Knossos, has become more formal. Two bright
frescoes that have a common theme show monkeys among flowers: known as the Blue
Monkey and the Crocus Gatherer or Saffron Gatherer, they are shown here. The
monkeys — unless the artist had merely seen them abroad — were presumably imported
from Egypt. These two frescoes also show another affinity, rather curious: there is a
habit of showing flowers and plants among a sort of formalized framework of rocks, as
if the scene was an underwater one; Evans notes the use of a decoration motif that gives
the impression of a sponge. Perhaps all we can say is that all is grist to the mill of an
artist who possesses Minoan exuberance.

The Minoan exuberance in pottery showed itself first in elaborate and exciting shapes.
There is a jug with a spout that makes one think that the maker must have seen a toucan
(plate 10), which is not likely. In truth this fondness for the bizarre did not altogether
disappear. There is the spined or prickled ware of the Middle Minoan II period, the
so-called barbitone type, of which an example is shown here; and the later Minoans
were rather addicted to what can only be called "trick" or facetious pottery, such as the
double jug illustrated overleaf, which can have had no conceivable advantage over a
single one. Perhaps the Minoans always liked "some new thing", as St Paul said rather
scornfully of their successors, the Athenians.*

*— though in another context — Acts 17, v. 21.

92

A Minoan jug in the barbitone style

The double jug, an example of Minoan
"trick" pottery

But there did come beauty. Early designs were mostly formal patterns of lines — not
incidentally to be confused with the ware specifically called "geometric", which was the
product of the island's Dorian Greek population of several hundred years later. This
gave way, first to a much freer patterning based on Nature and then to a complete,
though certainly not a photographic, naturalism. Harriet Boyd Hawes, one of the early
excavators in Crete, puts it this way:

> The Cretan potter's first appreciation of nature was subjective; not distinguishing clearly
> between himself and the world in which he moved. . . . The line left on the sand by receding
> waves, the ripple on water as the wind crossed it, the mysterious inner markings of a shell,
> the thousand varieties of spirals in shells and in tendrils, the shadow cast on his path by
> interlacing twigs, the stir of leaves and bending of branches, the flight of petals and seed-
> vessels, and the whirl which is at the basis of so many forms of motion, gathering particles

Naturalistic design of grasses
on a Minoan jug

to one focus and flinging them forth again—these attracted him. The artist was awakening to nature; his aim, however, was not to imitate what he saw but to record an impression, somewhat in the spirit of a Japanese artist.

But then:

At the height of his power the Minoan potter went direct to nature for his inspiration. His designs are full of grace and exuberance; reeds, grasses, and flowers adorn his vases; the life of the sea is represented with astonishing fidelity; but his naturalism is controlled by a rare power of selection and grouping. Some of his most charming patterns were painted on vases as thin as the egg-shell cups of Middle Minoan style (now usually called Kamares pottery (plate 10), from the cave where first discovered), others were executed on jars so heavy and coarse that no idea of their being decorated was at first entertained by the excavators. With a true instinct for beauty, he chose his favourite flowers, the lovely lily and iris, the wild gladiolus and crocus, all natives of the Mediterranean basin, and the last three, if not the lily, of his own soil.

He even beautifully decorated his flower-pots — if the pots with a hole in their base which Arthur Evans found were flower-pots, which seems a reasonable proposition.

There are two forms of art in which the Minoan does not seem to have excelled. The one is in soaring and imposing architecture; the other is in the lifesize or more than lifesize statue. The vast winged-bull portals of Assyria, the overwhelming colonnade of Karnak or the colossi of Abu Simbel are not for him. This fact may show a lack of achievement, but it also surely shows a trait, or rather traits, of character. Let us add, lest we seem to be straying only very slightly this side of idolatry, that the truth may not have been wholly admirable: just possibly a lightness of character as well as a healthy dislike of the portentous.

With these two exceptions the Minoans excelled in all the then known arts, and particularly perhaps in the small and the miniature. The man who painted the miniature frescoes must have had a beautiful time. Working as he was in a medium that required rapidity of execution, he boldly used or invented a convention that gave him full scope, the convention of using a swathe of colour for the watching crowd, brown for men, white for women, and of etching into it in lines of black or white, the suggestion of a mass of individual people. It *is* a crowd, and it is intently watching — especially the crowd in the scene of the "sacred grove and dance", for in the rear people are throwing up their arms with enthusiasm. But the maleness of the men with their quiff or coxcomb is shown, and the women are very feminine. As for the pampered ladies in the best seats in the so-called Temple Fresco, when he comes to draw them the artist lets himself go. Here is indeed a conversation-piece to end all conversation-pieces. Here is a cartoon, perhaps a slightly malicious one at that (see page 60).

In carving, both in the small and in the miniature, the Minoan often showed a high seriousness, or at least does so in what is left to us. The Harvester Cup (pages 13 and 22), carved in the soft stone called steatite, manages most successfully, in the difficult medium of semi-solid relief, to create the illusion of depth and perspective. Some consider the sistrum player to have been a priest and the procession may be a religious one; nevertheless it is a very cheerful occasion.

Other carving in steatite is shown on a tall conical *rhyton* or pourer such as the youth in the Cup Bearer fresco is carrying. It shows various sports; and sports with the Minoans as with the Greeks were always no doubt part of a religious festival. Here is boxing, and with one set of boxers wearing protective helmets, perhaps a more civilized manner of conducting the sport than the modern world has yet achieved. Here also is wrestling and bull-leaping. All the panels show a terrific verve and feeling for movement.

Another rhyton, the bull's-head (plate 11), would not have pleased the functionalist if any had existed at that time or those who object to any article of use being made unnecessarily in the shape or likeness of something else. But the Minoans, like all their Bronze Age contemporaries, were not here thinking in terms of the sweet or charming

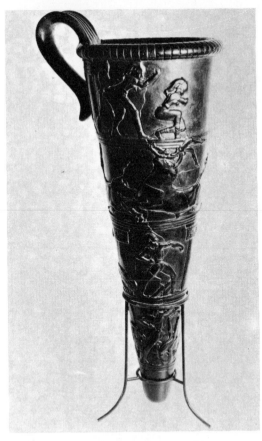

The Hagia Triada rhyton

but of the symbolic. This delicate and beautiful thing, eight inches high without the horns, was found in the villa, or possibly chapel, called the "little palace" at Knossos and is one of the most striking works of art discovered. It too is carved from steatite, but the gilded horns were of wood, the white band round the nostrils is of shell, and the eyes — very realistic — are of rock crystal, the iris painted black and the pupil red.

Was this strange and striking container used to pour a libation to the earth goddess, was it passed round, equally ceremoniously, at a feast? The liquid, poured in at the back of the neck, came out of the mouth. One cannot avoid thinking of the later (or later-lasting) rites of Cybele and of Mithras. If the liquid was red wine, were those who watched, or those who drank, reminded of the red blood? And if the wine spilt over the face, was there an awed, and to us gruesome, thrill? Certainly the rhyton would have been handled with more respect and somewhat deeper feelings than those of the present-day hostess who pours from a teapot made with equal ingenuity into the like-ness of a pop singer or a pixie.

Of carving in the round, the ivory figurine of a leaping or diving youth (plate 3) must obviously be concerned with some form of sport or acrobatics. Some think he is performing the bull-leap over the animal's horns, some that he is jumping down on to a bull's back to help catch it. He may of course be doing neither, though he was found next to the fragments of faience bulls. Arthur Evans says that the remains of two other leaping youths were among the debris, but unfortunately they were too far gone to be

97

repaired; even this remaining youth had to have his waist reconstituted in wax, which explains probably why he is not shown with the usual Minoan metal girdle. All the limbs, both of those in fragments and of the mended figure, show great attention to detail, not only of muscle but of outstanding veins. The whole effect of the completed figure is one of tremendous verve.

One aspect of the little figure — it extends to something just under a foot in length — may however disconcert us a little; it shows, once again, very much a romantic rather than a classical taste. It is that the head is bored to take gold-wire imitation of hair, tresses that no doubt were made to fly out behind, to give an added impression of speed and movement.

Clay figures, common finds in Crete, display a more homely touch. They are the poor man's votive offering, or household charm, or ornament, and are usually pretty crude. The one reproduced here shows some refinement. The lady is usually described as in a praying attitude. But the traditional Minoan praying attitude is of both arms raised above the head, and this seems more a stance of respectful adoration.

The art of faience, or of coating clay with glaze, may have been learnt from Egypt but was enthusiastically developed in ancient Crete. Its results are not often found except at the palace of Knossos, which thus seems to be shown as the seat of the industry, another intimation that the great sprawling entities of the palaces were the homes of craftsmen as well as courtiers. In faience was made anything from simple beads to elaborate figurines. Two of the less well known pieces that have been found show a gentle love of nature. One portrays a cow lovingly bending its head to lick its calf, and the other, a wild goat suckling its young. The much more famous faience figures are of the "snake goddess".

There are three of these. One now resides in the Boston (U.S.A.) museum and no one knows when or whether it was discovered in Crete. (It is shown on page 66.) Arthur Evans accepted it as genuine; and since it shows a difference from the other two in that the snakes are portrayed in metal, an aberration which is surely the last thing a forger would have thought of creating, we may be pretty sure that the master was right, though it is not fashionable nowadays always to think him so. Both the other two found by Evans himself, in one of the underground "safe-deposits" or treasuries and no one certainly has dared to question the authenticity of these. Their dress is elaborate, and as we have already pointed out, in line with that of the ladies of the palace; their hats or head-dresses are imposing and elaborate — one has the emblem of a lion or leopard perched on her head — and whether they represent goddesses or priestesses is open to question, though majority opinion inclines to the former. The implications of playing with snakes, as those of playing with bulls, are considerable, and will be discussed in a later chapter. The larger of these two figures, the one with the tall hat — they are about fourteen and twelve inches high respectively — has something of a naïve and pathetic appearance; the other is stern, dedicated and almost fierce.

Finally there is the work in metal and in precious stones. Crete was by tradition the birthplace of metal-working; yet the finds in the island of works of art made in metal have not been great, nowhere near so many as in Mycenaean Greece. The probable reason for this has been explained by one who knows Crete and its ancient history well, Professor Spyridon Marinatos, one-time Ephor of Cretan Antiquities. He says:

Clay figure of a woman, found at Piskokephalo in Sitia, eastern Crete

One of the two faience snake goddesses from the palace of Knossos

Faience figure of cow licking its calf, from the palace of Knossos

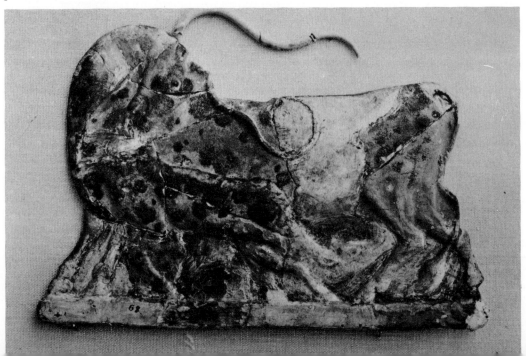

The answer that there are no unplundered tombs in Crete is inadequate. More probably the difference lies in the different ways of life in Greece and Crete. The Mycenaean warrior collected riches not for his pleasure on earth but, like the Egyptian, to take with him to the other world (and, we might add, for prestige). Minoan Crete had no warriors, and the riches accumulated in a life of peace were not so considerable. The Minoan lived for the present; he provided himself and his family with all comforts, with rich and artistically fashioned furnishing, but was satisfied with clay, stone and bronze as materials. He took few of his belongings with him into the other world.*

No gold masks, therefore, such as rejoiced the heart of Schliemann at Mycenae. There are however gold necklaces and ornaments in no way inferior to anything found on the Greek mainland, and bronze lamps and shallow bowls. The Linear B tablets give us a clue to these last: they are table ware, probably finger-bowls, which are by no means a modern luxury and feature in Homer. Miniature golden emblems of the double axe are not uncommon. The greatest find was at Mallia, of a gold pendant about two inches across, showing what is usually interpreted as two hornets holding a honeycomb, though a more reasonable interpretation would either deny the honeycomb or substitute bees for hornets. This is surely a girl's ornament for adornment, not a priestess's for ritual. If it is hornets, a countryman will tell you that these insects are really much better tempered than bees — which fact the Minoans no doubt knew.

This gold ornament dates from comparatively early times, about 2000 B.C. The signet rings and seals made from gems (plate 13) begin even earlier, and for a practical reason. The seal is the authenticity mark, the equivalent of the personal signature of the ancient world. The Sumerians made it in the shape of a cylinder, often formed around a pin that may have been worn for convenience in the hair — one king is said to have been done to death by such a bare bodkin. The Minoans preferred less deadly or less utilitarian ornaments in their hair and favoured seals with a flat surface that were either inset into a finger ring or made into the shape of little prisms, the flat surface being incised with the design and the other two surfaces being slightly concave in order to fit into finger and thumb. (Many may be seen in the Minoan room of Oxford's Ashmolean Museum, and repay as long a study as inevitable eye-strain will allow: short sight, such as Arthur Evans is said to have had, is an advantage in looking at seals.)

The seal, of course, needed work of the utmost minuteness and delicacy; and the Minoans excelled in it. Nor was the lens invented to help the unmyopic eye. Curiously enough, the seal that showed hieroglyphic signs — the most obvious equivalent of a signature — appears early but disappears later. The important people of Minoan Crete in its time of greatness apparently preferred something more highly artistic, though no doubt always highly individual and also highly symbolic. Perhaps the seals had become more talismans than signatures. They were such personal possessions that they did sometimes find their way into the grave with their owner — and sometimes even did survive the tomb robber, a person incidentally no commoner in Crete than anywhere else.

One of the most beautifully worked signet rings — it measures very nearly an inch across — shows the priestesses or dancers, with the deity obligingly floating down from

* From *Crete and Mycenae* (London, 1960)

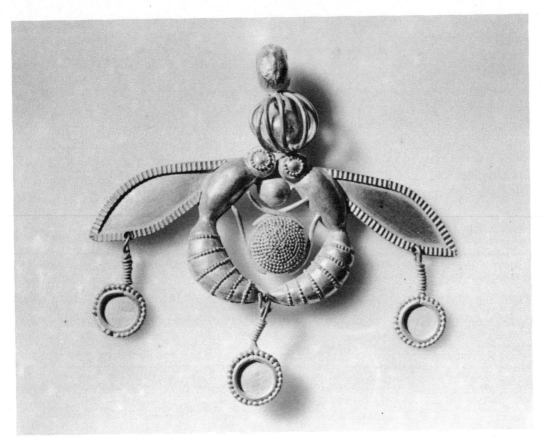

Above. Gold pendant from Mallia: "two hornets holding a honeycomb"

Below. Gold signet ring showing ladies tending fruit trees

above, that we have already referred to in connection with Minoan dress (plate 14). Another signet ring of the same size (page 101) — a cumbersome thing to wear on the finger, though not outlandishly so — shows other bare-breasted ladies, with more natural heads, dancing amid and tending the fruit trees, again no doubt with religious and talismanic import. The small-headedness on the former seal is no doubt intentional — the ladies may even be meant to be griffin-headed — and as time goes on the seals do tend to become more stylized, or it would be fairer to say more mannered. A bull-leaper is shown — he seems to be vaulting sideways and the bull is lying down — and animals are often portrayed. A favourite scene is of a lion attacking a deer, and this is one that the Roman mosaic workers also favoured, a mosaic at Verulamium even showing the lion carrying away the stag's head. Was this scene in real life so striking — appalling would be too strong a word to use where Bronze Age people were concerned — that it lasted in men's thoughts through a couple of millennia? Even the Cretan himself is likely to have copied it from a mainland artist, since, as we know, Hercules, or somebody, had cleared his island of lions, if indeed they were ever there. There is hardly reason in this to imagine the Minoan as a sadistic person. Rather it is another example of his love of portraying action.

The Minoan artist, one feels, was a realist — his bull-leaping or bull-catching scenes are almost as likely to portray accident as achievement. But he was also a sentimentalist, that is to say if to portray idyllic scenes is sentimental. He was unlike most of his contemporaries in the Bronze Age world: he liked to portray vital nature and natural vitality, and was allowed to do so; he hated to portray stiff formality and the portentous, and was not forced into it.

Seal-stone showing sideways bull-leap

Chapter Eight

THE THOUGHTS OF THE PEOPLE

Art in the ancient world is the great give-away. It shows those that follow after what men thought and felt and believed. It may do so elliptically, obliquely, enigmatically; but the information is there if the searcher can fill in the gap, discover the slant, appreciate the allusion.

Let us take the frescoes on the sides of the limestone sarcophagus found in a chamber tomb near to the palace of Hagia Triada. It dates from about 1400 B.C. — an ominous date, incidentally, when death was in the air. The frescoes are full of action as ever. But they are full of symbolism too. They show funerary rites.

The sarcophagus is a sturdy thing with thick legs and its length is about four and a half feet. Allowing for wide border-patterns therefore, the panels on each of the long sides measure about a yard by ten and twelve inches respectively and the end panels are roughly a foot square. Into each of these not very large panels the artist has crowded a great deal; he has painted in tones of buff, sienna and a greeny-blue.

We will first take note of what is portrayed as objectively as possible. First the slightly

The Hagia Triada sarcophagus, first side

narrower and more perfect panel. It is divided into three scenes. On the left a bare-headed woman wearing what looks like a sheepskin skirt is pouring liquid from a large vase into what we may legitimately call a mixing bowl. This bowl is raised up and stands between two columns bearing at their head the duplicated emblem of the double axe, and on the axes are perched two birds. A second woman follows carrying two more vases or buckets, and she is followed by a man playing a large lyre. The woman wears a head-dress reminiscent of that worn by the man in the Young Prince fresco. The background now becomes greeny-blue and the scene changes. Three young men, also clad in sheepskin skirts, come bearing gifts: two calves, life-size and presumably alive, and something that may be taken as the model of a boat. Finally, against a white background again, a man stands very straight and still and upright, clad fully in a sheepskin cloak that envelops his arms. Behind him is what looks like his own sarcophagus, and before him are steps and a tree.

Now the other side. Here are four scenes, or at any rate four different backgrounds. On the left, where a large piece is missing, five pairs of feet suggest two pairs of women following a single one. This leader seems to be the same crowned figure as on the other side. She walks ceremoniously, holding her arms before her. Next comes an unmistakable sacrifice. A bound bull on an altar seems to watch sadly his own life blood drain away into a vessel below. Beside this vessel patiently wait two goats. Behind, a man plays on the double pipes. Next, a skirted woman, with the same gesture of outstretched arms

The Hagia Triada sarcophagus, second side

as the crowned one, rests her hands on an altar. Behind is the same double-axe stand and above the altar a jug and a bowl of fruit. Finally appears what looks like a large edition of the altar. Its top is edged with those formalized representations of bulls' horns known to the archaeologist as horns of consecration, and above it grows another tree.

The two end panels have a similarity and a difference. In both two people, pale-faced, are driving a chariot. But in one they drive a stocky and homely horse; while in the other they are driving mythical creatures, splendidly winged griffins, and at the same time are facing a strange and menacing bird.

Interpretation is not easy: one can make almost what one likes of it — which is of course the danger. There is not even any way of telling to what extent, if any, the scenes interconnect. But other relics of a religious nature can help us, as can a knowledge of Bronze Age ways of thought in general; and we will give what seem the most reasonable and accepted explanations. We shall be led, conveniently, into a more general consideration of Minoan beliefs.

The most likely explanation of the sarcophagus scenes as a whole is a simple one. Here is a man — the figure in the sleeveless cloak — watching his own funerary rites. There is first a libation to the Earth Goddess. It might be of wine, it might be of blood, it might be a mixture of the two; the mixing bowl may have a hole in it so that the liquid seeps down into the earth. There is a bearing of gifts, again either to the deity or deities, or to the dead man himself, for his succour in the world to come. There is a sacrifice,

The two end panels of the Hagia Triada sarcophagus

principally of a bull, and an offering of wine and the fruits of the earth at a sanctuary. As to the end panels, although it is the Minoan custom to show women as pale and men as brown, yet it is also a more universal creation to show also a dead man as pale. The griffin scene may therefore depict him flying off to heaven; and the bird may be an evil spirit trying to prevent him. The other panel might have that optimistic aspect common in Egyptian tombs, where the dead man is shown indulging in the heavenly equivalent of the activities he most delighted in on earth, fishing in the river or driving his chariot: the Minoan, having arrived, reverts to his more homely mode of transport, his buggy and mare.

The more we speculate, however, the more fanciful we are likely to become—though the sarcophagus does constitute a very human and very revealing document. What are really of more interest to us are the various religious symbols in the pictures, evidence of the meaning of which comes to us from other sources. Of course the sarcophagus, by its nature, tells us primarily of the rites of the dead; but it also has wider religious implications.

There are the trees, for instance, and the pillar supporting the double axe, and the birds on top.

Of the axes themselves it is enough to say that in ancient Crete no ceremony either royal or religious would have been complete without them: they are the power sign and the good luck sign. But why are they on pillars? It might be enough to dismiss the question by calling the pillars merely axe-stands. But pillars by themselves do keep on appearing at Knossos and elsewhere, and both in representation and in actuality. They appear in the crypts of the palaces and villas, and what is most significant they are not necessarily pillars that support anything: they are cut off before reaching the ceiling. In effigy the apparently functionless but obviously highly symbolic pillar even travels across to Mycenae, to form the central feature of the headstone above the famous lion gate. There must have been a pillar cult.

A pillar seems a strange and uninspiring thing to worship, or at least, if that is too strong a word, to regard with awe as symbolic and pregnant with meaning. Two explanations are possible; and both give us a little insight into the minds of the Minoans. A third, very general, explanation is possible, the wide one, that is to say, that great upstanding stones in all ways and in all places have impressed the primitive mind. Such is by no means necessarily a phallic idea; a great stone, particularly after someone has troubled to set it upright, is impressive. The Bronze Age Minoan was admittedly not primitive; but he may have seen cause to carry through the predilection to his own more sophisticated times. The first of the two more specific explanations takes us to caves, of which a famous one is in Mount Ida, as already mentioned, and another near to the port of Knossos and called Eilythyia. There are two points about these caves. They saw the dawn of Cretan neolithic religion, having been in fact left fairly cluttered with votive offerings. Secondly, there are inside them natural pillars, stalagmites and stalactites. In the flickering light of a torch these glistening natural pillars would look most impressive. And it is the impressive thing, the thing that sets the eyes starting or the heart lifting or the skin pricking, which becomes the religious symbol: it has, in a word, *mana*, power from above. The other explanation connects pillars with trees, for which there is much evidence of Cretan high regard. The ideal tree may become simplified into a

The cave of Eilythyia, near the port of
Knossos

pillar, just as the real tree had its branches lopped off and its base up-ended and became a real pillar in the palace.

But why pay such regard to a tree? Perhaps the question does not need to be answered. There are few more impressive natural objects than a great tree; it also in many forms bears fruit pleasant to man and beast. Early men all over the world worshipped trees: Sir James Frazer in that monumental collation of atavistic beliefs, *The Golden Bough,* fills two-thirds of a column of index on the subject. As for Crete itself, there is the signet ring already shown to illustrate the presence of the cult in the island, as there is the miniature fresco that portrays the dancers dancing in a grove of trees. Once again, too, the idea travels over the sea to Mycenaean Greece, in the shape of the so-called ring of Nestor, found at Pylos. This in so many ways shows its Cretan origin and style, as it shows a multiplicity of symbols, and a tree and its branches form a framework for the whole theme.

Now a people who hold trees in reverence and who among trees perform their ritual ceremonies, whose temple is in fact a grove of trees, are likely to be a relatively free-minded and open-hearted people in their religion, not unduly overrun or overawed by priests, since at least the priest is always likely to build himself a real temple to enhance his importance. Ancient Crete is indeed distinctive in leaving behind no temples, no great cult statues, no monumental, brooding statues of a deity.

It left behind instead a small thing, the miniature likeness of a woman. In neolithic times it is the frank and crude representation of the woman with big belly and generous breasts; in later times it is the woman in command of her symbolic creature companions, the snake, the lion, the bull, the dove. She is the great goddess of Nature and Fertility, the Great Earth Mother. It is a simple and single idea. To quote Marinatos again:

> The original deity in Crete, with its uniquely peaceful culture and united population, was not known in many different forms. There was no need for a war-god, there were no independent areas or peoples who had invented their own deities, there was no lively mythology of religion which demanded a plurality of gods. The island's possessions, the people's loves and fears, were for their fields and herds, for which they entreated fertility, their woods and mountains in which they hunted, the sea which they held in awe, the earthquake from the depth which they rightly dreaded. In these circumstances they naturally worshipped their deity as nature goddess, huntress, queen of animals, sea goddess, earth goddess.

In other words the Minoans worshipped one single goddess but in many aspects, or emanations.

Before we consider these aspects, however, one thing must be made clear. There are, it has sometimes been said, really only two early religions, an earth worship and a sun worship. And the former, it is held, is both a more primitive and a darker religion. It came from the first farmers, who in leaving behind a hunting economy made themselves both more dependent upon and more intimate with the earth. They saw that there was a death and a rebirth of Nature each year, and they saw too that death, and blood, could quite literally revivify the earth and the produce of the earth. There grew up therefore that great corpus of belief in human sacrifice and the influence of sacrifice, especially the influence of the sacrifice of the great ones: "the king must die!" There is, however—and this is the point—little evidence of this darker side of the earth religion among the Minoans. There is no evidence whatever of human sacrifice, not always easy to recognize, admittedly, but often quite obvious as when a skeleton is discovered beside a foundation stone. There is mention in myth of an eight-year cycle for the kings of both Crete and Greece. But King Minos by tradition did not die; instead he sojourned to the top of Mount Ida, and there, like Moses with the tablets of the law, emerged from the sacred cave refreshed by communion with the divinity.

In one Minoan seal the goddess herself is shown triumphant upon a mountain top. This is one of the occasions when she is shown with attendant lions, an unexpected beast for her to have communion with and therefore perhaps foreign in origin. The fact that another Minoan seal shows similarly a male figure with lions rather strengthens this probability: he is "master of the beasts", in the same way as the Sumerian hero Gilgamesh is shown literally twisting the lion's tail. The goddess-with-the-doves seems an idea much more likely to be indigenous to Crete—and is in fact much more commonly shown.

To regard birds as omens is a natural thing to do, natural that is to say if one is continually looking for omens, as all Bronze Age people no doubt were: birds fly up so startlingly and move so unpredictably. Bird as embodiment of spirit is a natural idea too —if for no other reason than that birds fly *up*. So in ancient Crete the bird—and in representation it usually looks like a dove—is often a companion of the goddess. It seems also to be something more, a manifestation of the goddess, her epiphany. So to the Minoan imagination the bird alights—and blesses by her presence. So in the Hagia

Seal showing Minoan goddess upon a mountain top

Triada scene she alights on the pillared effigy of the double axe—and as it were makes double blessedness thrice blessed. When the world was young, divinity was more easily visible to man, and apparently not least so in Crete. Once more to quote the man who knows the beloved island so well, Spyridon Marinatos:

> In a warm country like Crete, where the temperature and imagination of the people were easily stirred by religious and intensified by natural phenomena, men readily saw visions and dreamed dreams. Even today, in the gloom of the caves, the peasants discern the forms of men and animals among the shadows and pinnacles of rock. The incredibly clear atmosphere in spring and autumn produces mirages which set seas and fields floating in the air. Strange reflections over the Cretan valleys . . . throw shadows like men on to the skies. In those days gods were more ready to show themselves to mortals; Homer knew this well. Specific rituals, prayers, dances, offerings, could conjure up the god and even dismiss him. So we must suppose that the god of the Minoans not only lived beneath the ground, in caves, in woods and on mountains, but also ascended to the heavens.

No one, it might be added, in seeking to interpret the ways of thought and imagination of the peoples of the distant past, must expect to meet consistency.

The snake as a familiar of the goddess is completely earthy. This connection may not be immediately apparent to modern men, particularly to those only acquainted with snakes in the brightly lit cubicles of zoos. But the creature does certainly keep as close to the earth as possible, and does in his sudden silent appearances and disappearances seem to arrive out of and return into the earth—some kinds, indeed, make their homes in holes in the ground. The snake has, too, that aspect of startlingness, of the uncanny, that is necessary for a phenomenon to impress primitive man and to be credited with god-given powers. So therefore the goddess with her snakes about her, or—for we may interpret either way—the priestess imitating the goddess and exerting similar powers.

What is significant about Minoan regard for the snake is that it seems to have been mostly a private and personal regard. The creature not only acts as the familiar of the goddess, symbolic of her chthonic or earthly powers, but, because of that symbolism, is also itself a power to be encouraged or appeased. The rich man in his villa, the poor man in his hut, each seems to have had his hole for the pet and tutelary snake to appear from, and a bowl of offering beside the hole—again a custom not unknown in other climes and other and more recent times. The Minoans, however, in their kindness and from their powers of observation coupled with their sanitary efficiency, seem to have gone one step further. Noting that the snake liked to hide in their drain-pipes the ancient Cretans actually made clay tubes in which their snakes could live—that that was their purpose is proved by the discovery of models showing snakes crawling up into these homes. The idea, in spreading to the Cypriots and later to the Philistines, seems curiously to have combined itself with the dove cult, the tube being converted, in one such model, to be also a dovecot, with doves perched on the handle or the dove-goddess peeping out of a hole. There must have been something more than symbolism in all this, with the snake regarded as a guardian of the home, which in practice and in the way of keeping down vermin it may very well have been. Regard for the snake, however, must have been an ambivalent one, a love-hate relationship, for even man's predecessor the monkey cannot abide a snake. If priestesses of the Mother Goddess let snakes slither about their persons, then the multitude, even an unsqueamish Bronze Age multitude, must surely have watched with a slightly sickened fascination. . . .

If doves were beneficent—as surely they were, those most mutually faithful and loving creatures—there is also to be reckoned with the bird on the end panel of the Hagia Triada sarcophagus, which looks far from beneficent. We must believe that the Minoans had their demons—what ancient people did not? The most unequivocal representation of demons is on a fresco at Mycenae, done that is to say on the orders of a Greek but no doubt executed by a Minoan. The demons appear to be doing useful work, as in Egypt they sometimes did; and, as was usual, they have animals' heads. What is not quite so usual, and what might be indicative of a somewhat carefree attitude to the subject, is that they have in this instance the heads of donkeys. Other examples of Minoan theramorphism, of inventing strange beasts, of putting animal heads on to people, are not, we must admit, so light-hearted in their imputation, as will be seen in the next chapter but one.

The kindly, homely, comforting divinity of the ancient world is usually a trinity, the holy family of mother, father and son. Crete shows little sign of that. There are, however, the figures of what has come to be known as the Boy God. There is also the later Greek assertion that the greatest of their gods, Zeus, was born in a cave in Crete, even that he died in one too. Whether the Minoans ever knew a god whom they called Zeus it is impossible to say. But there is likely to be some reason for the tradition; and it is highly significant that the Greek Zeus was son of the Earth Mother.

The Linear B tablets come into the argument again here—we promised that we should return to them. There is a series of tablets discovered at Knossos that give lists of monthly offerings—usually of olive oil—to the deities of various shrines. The fact of these offerings is itself of interest, as showing something of a centrally directed religion even if there existed no temples and few priests. But the names of the recipients are more interesting, though some of the transliterations may be a little questionable. The Priestess of the Winds appears, and All the Gods; also Poseidon and the Earth-shaker. One entry seems to refer to the cave of Eilythyia and one to "the Dictean Zeus". But it must be remembered that these Linear B tablets were written by Greek-speaking (or Greek-writing) scribes; and what was Zeus to the scribe was probably not Zeus to the Minoan common man. However, that there was a male god in Crete, and also many gods, does not seem unlikely. Nor is this statement necessarily a contradiction of what has gone before. For no Bronze Age religion was strictly monotheistic, and though each holy place is likely to have had its god or goddess these are also likely to have been no more than local variants and pale shadows of the central divinity. It was the Greeks who multiplied their gods, giving them not local importance but particular attributes. And with the attributes went sometimes the ancient symbolic companions, perhaps taken from Crete: Aphrodite had the dove; and visitors to the Acropolis of Athens may still see the crypt where was kept the serpent sacred to Athena. But the whole question of the connections between Minoan and later Greek religion is a difficult one and one in which it is all too easy to become lost in the labyrinths of mythology and comparative theology. We will be content to observe that the central Cretan Earth Mother is not dethroned. She is, rather, supported—though of course supporters can sometimes try to usurp.

One symbol appearing on the Hagia Triada sarcophagus has not yet been touched

111

upon. It is the so-called horns of consecration. To give them such a name is really to presuppose their use and significance. Evans called them simply sacred horns; Marinatos contents himself with saying that though they are the best-known Minoan symbols they are not the best understood and that it can only be said that they represent the god himself or – more often – indicate the sanctity of a place. At times they seem to be not much more than the rather fussy ornamentation added to the parapet of a building, as the late Victorians used elaborate ridge-tiles – but even so, if you can use a sacred symbol for your decoration and, as it were, throw in a blessing free of charge, then so much the better.

It is indeed tempting to credit these Minoans, who in so many ways give the impression of themselves as gay and sophisticated and even heartless, as sometimes taking their religion a little lightly. But we must be circumspect with such an interpretation: not to be priest-ridden, not to be obsessed with the cult of the dead or the fear of demons, is different from being non-religious. Votive offerings, shrines and sanctuaries abounded in ancient Crete; at Mallia was found a great round stone, dimpled at its circumference, for the receiving of ritual gifts and known to the Greeks as a Kernos; the Hagia Triada sarcophagus so abounding in symbolism does show a high concern for the souls of the departed. Nor can we assume that priests did not exist. The gift-carriers on the sarcophagus are not necessarily priests, but they do wear the special sheepskin skirt.

The throne-room at Knossos, restored by
Sir Arthur Evans

One priest we may be fairly sure of, King Minos himself, for no Bronze Age king was not also chief representative of the God. To end this chapter seeking to understand the outlook of a people light-hearted yet fundamentally religious, we may return to the throne-room at Knossos, about which little was said at the time of describing the palace. It is an impressive though not a large room, and it was found with the frescoes on its walls more intact than anywhere else. These represent the fabulous griffins, lions with birds' heads, which also appear on the Hagia Triada sarcophagus: that they have a religious significance seems obvious, though what it was we cannot say. More easily translatable and more significant, is the fact that in front of the throne broad steps lead down to what Arthur Evans has called a lustral area, or place for ceremonial cleansing. The belief that such was its purpose—and these sunken areas often fitted with a drain occur similarly elsewhere—was in this instance supported by the presence of a jar for olive oil.

That this jar was found overturned may have another, and sinister, significance, to which we will return.

Chapter Nine

THE CRETANS AND THE BULL

The Minoan acrobat of the bullring, the bull-leaper, is an almost incredible figure. To those who know most about the bull he is the most incredible, for no modern gaucho or matador has dared to do what he is portrayed as doing, and many have declared it impossible. We must believe in him, however: the evidence is too strong to do otherwise.

He or she—to write "he-she" might be better, for if ever there was an epicene figure this is one—must have been a striking phenomenon. Mary Renault, in her novel of the Theseus legend, *The King Must Die*, has made of the bull-leaper a popular and idolized figure, equivalent of the modern pop singer or television star, but even more theatrical. And that is surely a justified interpretation. The closer equivalent would be the chariot racers of Imperial Rome—those stars of the racecourse, *miliarii* because they had won at least a thousand races, whose wealth was fabulous, whose likeness was known to every-one, and whose outrageous escapades were universally condoned. We may thus imagine the bull-leaper walking self-consciously within the courts or between the white houses of the streets of Knossos, waiting and expecting to be recognized. As the dashing cavalry officer will wear his spurs though he could walk more comfortably without them, so the bull-leaper will wear his anklet-gaiters. His loin-cloth will be immaculate and brightly painted or embroidered; his bracelets will be costly, his hair curled, his face perhaps, even out of the theatral ring, made up.

Nevertheless, he will be a brave man, or if a girl an even braver woman, for surely in any age it is not natural for the gentler sex, the child-bearing sex, to do such things.

First the bull-leaper will have to catch his bull. Or, if his skill is reserved for the ring, then someone of not much inferior skill will have to do the catching. There is a part of the bull scene on the second ring of the Hagia Triada rhyton that shows a man not neatly leaping the bull but in obvious difficulties, one would say in danger of his life. There is also the fragment of a painting on crystal that shows flying locks of human hair and also a rope above the bull. It seems most likely that both these scenes refer to the catching of a bull and not to the bullring. And—as has been said earlier—they bear such resemblance to a scene on one of the famous Vaphio cups that we surely cannot go wrong in believing that though these cups were found at a Mycenaean site they depict a Cretan happening; they are also in every way of Cretan shape and style of workmanship.

The scenes on these cups deserve close study. To what extent they represent a series of happenings or a single moment in time is hard to say; but quite obviously the pair of cups between them record the whole operation of bull-catching and a reasonably certain interpretation of them can be made.

On the first cup there is a tethered bull. We may legitimately imagine that he is a tame one, brought to lend authenticity to the scene. Then there is shown a bull intently following a scent, or what he sees, or both. Between these two creatures there is an amorous scene. But the cow, it is thought, is a decoy, manned no doubt as are our pantomime cows, and deftly worked. The bull—the same wild bull as we have seen approaching—is now being made into a fool. And he looks as if he were.

On the second cup the bull is netted. But he is a powerful beast and has no wish whatever to be caught. On the right of the netting scene, therefore, he is seen lashing out with his hind legs; on the left is a more terrifying scene. In this scene two men, or a man and a girl, risk their lives and exert all their skill in the capture. The one believed to be a girl is literally wrapping herself around the bull's horns to avoid annihilation.

Bull-hunting scene painted on a crystal plaque
(after a completed drawing in Evans: *Palace of Minos*)

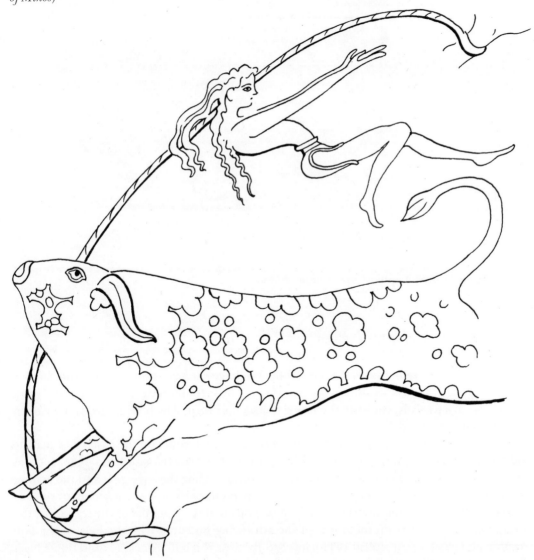

Scene from the first Vaphio Cup: a tethered bull

So much for the catching. Finally, after what training of the bull we do not know, after what intensive training of the bull-leapers we can only imagine, the great game and ceremony is ready to be shown to the public. We have the seal showing a less spectacular leap, a sort of sideways vault, but we have both a bronze statuette and a full-size fresco, as well as various seals, showing the more spectacular leap, which must surely have been the culmination of the show.

The bull-leap fresco (plate 12) was discovered in a small court on the eastern or private side of the palace of Knossos, part of a long frieze about thirty-two inches deep. It dates from about 1500 B.C. Because two figures are painted white they are girls and the bronze figure is a man. Whether between them they represent one scene at a moment of time or a series of scenes again is not clear. But it is obvious that the essential of the leap is for the performer to get between the horns of the advancing bull and, with the help of the bull itself if he is lucky or a skilful performer, to fly over the bull's neck, to land on its back

116

Plate 11. Steatite bull's-head rhyton or wine pourer, more symbolic than functional in design. The horns were of wood and have been renewed. *Photo: Holle Verlag*

Overleaf. Plate 12. The famous bull-leap fresco from Knossos, *c.* 1500 B.C.

Photo: Hirmer Verlag

Scene from the first Vaphio Cup: a cow used
as a decoy to catch the bull

and to vault off again, into the arms of an assistant. Some representations show the landing on the bull's back to be hands first, some show it to be feet first; one seal seems to
show a backwards somersault. All of these we may imagine to have been extremely
dangerous.

As to where the games were held, there is no clear evidence. At Knossos, the supposition is, on flat ground between the river and the private apartments. As was mentioned
earlier, one writer* favours the great central courtyard itself. His argument is that the
pillars of what are taken to be an altar or shrine or temple in the so-called "temple"
miniature fresco (and which give it its name) are similar to the remains of those found
in the west façade of the Knossos courtyard; and he adds that the central courts of

* James Walter Graham, in *The Palaces of Crete* (Princeton, N.J., 1962)

Knossos, Phaistos and Mallia are so remarkably similar as to lead one to suppose that they have been intentionally constructed to a formula, as is a tennis court. It has to be added that there is no sign as to what the crowd and the court ladies are watching (or singularly failing to watch) in the Temple Fresco. Indeed the very word "bullring" is an invention on the part of the archaeologist and the interpreters.

However, it is at least a highly reasonable invention. The bull-games must have been so spectacular, and they appear so often in Minoan art, that it is unthinkable that they were not performed before a crowd.

It is also true that all early peoples loved to gather in a crowd and that it is only a very modern trait, and perhaps an unnatural one, to feel anything different. Indeed it can be put more strongly and more significantly than that. All neolithic and Bronze Age people—and we have suggested that the peaceable Minoans were, in spite of their sophistication, nearer to the neolithic than some—all the primitive peoples loved to take part in a ceremony, loved to feel together the oneness of themselves under the aegis of their god. The existence of the bull-games—apart from the fact that they were bull-games and not some other sort of game—does not suggest an effete and idle population,

Scene from the second Vaphio Cup: the bull being netted

kept quiet by being given the equivalent of bread and circuses. It is much more likely to show a population united and religious.

Yet how dangerously misleading that word "religious" can be, especially to those who are heirs to anything like a puritanical tradition. To be religious was not of course to fail to be gay—indeed we may admit that the Minoans may have taken the gaiety a good distance and forgotten sometimes the religion. All sports in the ancient world, at least in the Aegean world, were connected with some religious ceremony; they were in fact themselves a ceremony, in honour of the god, in honour of the dead. The same can be said, and even more so, of the dance; and the Minoans went down in legend as famous for their dancing. Leaving the bull and the bull-games for a moment, we shall do well to consider the dance as an indication of Minoan character and institutions. Nothing produces better than dancing a feeling of gaiety and excitement—and ecstasy. Rhythm is more potent than all the kings and captains, music than any edict or any bronze Talos striding the countryside. The Minoans had the lyre and the flute, and the sistrum with which to mark the time—see again the Hagia Triada sarcophagus and also the Harvester Cup. Evans believes that the river-flats east of the Knossos palace may have been a great dancing place, as well as the more formal "theatral area"; and he says that he has often

Scene from the second Vaphio Cup: a man and
girl risk their lives to capture the bull

stood to listen to a modern shepherd, homeward bound with his goats, pausing there to play his pipe:

> Those eerie notes hardly fail to wake more distant echoes in the listeners' ears and the magic spot calls up visions of the festal scenes once enacted on the level flat below—shut in, beyond, by the murmuring stream—where the immemorial olive-trees still spread their boughs. Fitfully, in the early summer, there float and poise in the sunny spaces between the trees swallow-tail butterflies, saffron, tinged with blue, like the robes of the dancers on the fresco, as if they were in truth the "little souls" of those gay ladies.

All of this does not mean that the Minoans were no more than a pleasure-loving people. That "gay lady" with her curls flying may well have ended her dance in such an ecstasy that she sank down at the end into unconsciousness. It means rather that the Minoans took their pleasure seriously—or, if that conjures up a picture of English phlegm and gloom on even the most riotous of occasions, let us say that they took their seriousness pleasantly.

What, sociologically, is of great importance in both the dance and the bull-games is that the first is always shown performed by women and the second performed equally by women as by men. There is no equivalent of King David dancing before the Ark of the Covenant.

There is in fact no equivalent of King David at all. Where in all the seals and figures and frescoes is King Minos? The "Prince" in the lily field with his peacock crown is the nearest to a royal figure, but it is we and not the Minoans who dubbed him prince, and in fact he was probably one of a procession of youths, no doubt noble but not necessarily royal and certainly not *the King*. That no king does ever seem to be shown does not of course deny his existence; he may have been too holy to have been pictured. What is truly significant is not what is lacking but what is very much present. Women are constantly pictured; women must therefore have been important in ancient Crete.

Can we go so far as to call the Minoan way of life a matriarchy? There is not enough evidence for that, and we must not forget that really the most documented fact about the Minoans is that they had a king called Minos. He may well, however, as in Egypt, have owed his kingship to the female line, that is to say, to a marriage to the princess. It may even be that in the dim past he was regarded as little more than the ritual fertilizer of the Queen Mother and that his retirement to the Dictean cave was not for spiritual regeneration but for immolation to make way for his successor. Such things may have happened in the dim past of any Mediterranean people. What is important is that by all the signs the ancient Cretans worshipped a Mother Goddess and that this was, as it were, rather an old-fashioned thing to do, at least so wholeheartedly. In the beginning men must have regarded women with a worshipful awe just because they performed that miracle of reproducing their kind. But slowly, and at varying speeds, men with their superior strength and drive took the initiative in all ways except the way in which they could not compete, even to the extent of deserting female divinity for male. The Minoans, at least we can say, were laggards in losing their awed regard for women.

What effects the undoubted importance of women and the possible lingering supremacy of women may have had in Crete it is not very easy to say: mostly the evidence is only negative. That there exists so little evidence of having gloried in military might could well be attributed to the gentleness of women; or possibly, which comes to nearly the same thing, the islanders' ability to lead a peaceful existence gave women a chance to make their gentleness felt. That female supremacy would lead to strict rules of male morality seems probable. But then most Bronze Age peoples and all primitive peoples had strict rules of sexual morality—and pretty harsh punishments, incidentally, on the occasions when custom and tradition proved insufficient deterrent against sin. That there was love of children, and so a liking to portray them, we may infer from two works of art left to us: the baby deedily playing on the floor, and a fragment of fresco showing older children doing the same thing. But then, again, most primitive people are kind to their young children. All we are really saying is that the Minoans had not been spoilt.

The participation of girls in the bull-games is of course the reverse of an aspect of female gentleness. It may have been a relic of female supremacy coupled with a sort of *noblesse oblige*. Some commentators have affected to see a family likeness in the features of the priestesses depicted, the Hagia Triada ones included: if Ariadne was the holy one and the king's daughter was the priestess, then perhaps the ladies of royal family always schooled themselves to do the significant and symbolic and also the unpleasant jobs—from playing with snakes to playing with bulls.

We are back with the bull and the bull-games. And of course "playing" is really an inadequate, if not indeed an insulting, word to use: "exerting their powers over" is a better expression. We may be sure that the bull-leap had its high symbolism and its religious significance.

What the symbolism and the significance were it is again not easy to imagine, though it is important to try to do so. We have some clues to help us. It brings us to serious, and unhappy, things.

The Minoans did not worship the bull. Rather, the bull was the most significant form of sacrifice to the Earth Mother, significant because it was the most impressive in the sight of the donor, and, he hoped, the most acceptable in the sight of the recipient. That the bull should impress man is easily seen: its size and power and potency would impress anyone. The connection between bull and earth is not so obvious.

Arthur Evans in his later excavations came across a small house at Knossos that had been ruined by huge blocks hurled down some twenty feet. Not only so, but in the basement of another nearby house, also ruined by earthquake and filled in with rubble, were the skeleton heads of two great bulls, "the horn-cores of one of which was over a foot in girth at the base". Evans drew his own conclusion: "The methodical filling in of the building and its final relinquishment as a scene of human habitation had been preceded by a solemn expiatory offering to the Powers below." And those powers he was himself twice to experience. Once was as his workmen were finishing the clearance of this very house, when all experienced "a short sharp shock, sufficient to throw one of my men backwards, accompanied by a deep rumbling sound". The other experience came to him while reading in bed in the Villa Ariadne, which was the house he had built for himself upon the site. He elected to see the shock through without leaving the building, which he deemed sufficiently strong. "But it creaked and groaned, and rocked from side to side as if the whole must collapse. Small objects were thrown about, and a pail, full of water, was nearly splashed empty. . . . A dull sound rose from the ground like the muffled roar of an angry bull."

125

Was *that* the connection between the bull and the Earth Mother? Arthur Evans thought it was. He remembered that Poseidon was a maker of earthquakes as well as a sea god to the Greeks and that there is a line in Homer, "In bulls does the Earth-shaker delight." Here then was a most unbeneficent power of the Earth Goddess, a roaring and earth-shaking bull which she kept below the ground and occasionally unleashed. So therefore the Minoans sacrificed live bulls to her; so they pitted their strength and their wits against the bull; so perhaps, in their "lustral areas", which were always underground, they performed expiatory rituals, rituals so important that the king himself would at times perform them.

Ideas sometimes grow by what they feed on and become obsessions. So perhaps in her last days of greatness the Minoans were obsessed by the bull. Perhaps they swore by him, daringly or idly according to the nature of the swearer. Perhaps the bull-leaper, if no more than handsome idol to the court ladies, was more the equivalent of St George to the common people. Perhaps, even, "the Bull" sounded in Minoan ears as "the Bomb" sounds in ours.

Chapter Ten

THE LAST PERIOD OF
GREATNESS

All things change, as the earliest of the Greek philosophers was to observe. No one can bathe in the same stream twice, for the water moves on. No one, not even the Cretans, can bathe indefinitely in the warm and sunlit waters of prosperity. For time moves on; and at some time, the gods, or the barbarians without, or both, will be jealous.

Here was a people protected by the sea; rich in flocks and in the fruits of a friendly earth; rich from trade, too; vital and vivid, uninhibited in their art, comfort-loving but active and athletic, pleasure-loving but pious and respectful to their god. Their civilization was to end, and be forgotten. Before it did so it would change: to a contemporary, her last fifty years of greatness may have seemed greatest of them all, but to hindsight there is, rather, a hint of over-ripeness and decadence. For the best part of 500 years, from about 1900 to 1450 B.C., for fifteen generations or more, Minoans had been enjoying a little-changing Bronze Age existence of the more peaceful kind. Then – if our dates are correct – great change had come, and after it, before a single span of human lifetime had ended, disaster.

What caused the disaster? How great was it? What connection with it had the fifty years of changed ways after the date 1450? Those are the questions that need answering – and to which it is possible only to give a tentative answer.

Two facts stand out. The first is that the fifty years are those in which the government at Knossos was keeping its accounts and archives in an early form of Greek, as were also the Mycenaeans. The second is that the Minoans were afraid of earthquakes and suffered from earthquakes. The two are interconnected.

The Mycenaeans first. At one time it was thought that only the Minoans influenced the Mycenaeans. Now we know that it was a mutual affair. Or rather, perhaps, it was a changing affair: the Minoans came first on the Aegean scene and first influenced the later-arriving and less civilized Mycenaeans; then gradually the tables were turned. And "influence" may be a euphemistic word to use.

Who were these Mycenaeans? So far, we have been a little chary of bringing them into the Cretan picture: they used the Linear B script, we said, exactly as they did at Knossos, but it would be dangerous to describe Minoan life from the evidence of the Mycenaean tablets. That was reasonable, because the Mycenaeans were a very different people from the Minoans. But now the situation is changed for we wish to understand Crete during its years of Mycenaean occupation – or, if that is not the right word, under Mycenaean influence, or dynastic hegemony.

The Mycenaeans were the first Greeks to arrive in Greece. They were one part of those Aryan-speaking peoples, largely blond and big, horse-using, who came from the steppe lands north of the Black and the Caspian seas. They also came into Asia Minor and into

India and wherever they came they changed the shape of history. They must have been masterful men.

They introduced the horse as a domesticated animal into the eastern Mediterranean world.

That in itself is a fact of significance. The horse is a wonderful creature: not very intelligent, they say, but able to change the men who use him. Men attach him to a chariot. They listen to him neighing—"he saith among the trumpets, Ha, ha; and he smelleth the battle afar off, the thunder and the captains, and the shouting." The men who use him become horsy men, who are different men.

With the coming of Linear B the Minoan world for the first time talks of chariots and horses. It becomes part of the Bronze Age chariot-using world, which is a militaristic world. As the golden chariot was found dismantled and packed in the tomb of Tutankhamen, weak scion of a dynasty of warrior pharaohs, so the Knossos tablets speak of: "One horse-chariot, painted crimson, dismantled", and "Three horse-chariots without wheels, inlaid with ivory, fully assembled, equipped with bridles with cheek-straps, decorated with ivory and horn bits". They are rich, and costly, and grand, these chariots; and they wait in the king's store-room, or they are brought out, and fitted together; and the restive, champing steeds are manoeuvred each side of the shaft, for the use perhaps of that great military figure, the king's Follower—and the little Cretans watch in wonder while the big Nordic groom controls them—and laugh behind their hands, perhaps, when he fails to do so. . . .

Now this is supposing that the Cretans and the Cretan rulers only became warlike after the Mycenaeans arrived at Knossos.

To an extent this is an over-simplification, but only to an extent. There is, for instance, the evidence of the wearing of daggers, given by votive offerings that show the weapon much in evidence. But call the dagger a knife, and half at least of the implication vanishes: people who have bronze are not going to go without a cutting tool. More

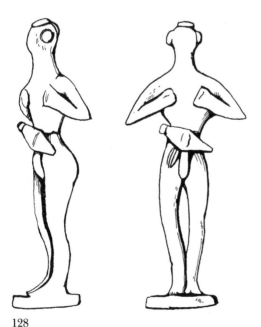

Clay figurine with a dagger, from Sitia in eastern Crete

specific is another steatite vase from Hagia Triada, known as the Chieftain's Cup. Here a long-haired, confident-looking and highly decorated young man seems to be giving commands to an "officer" who shoulders a bare sword and stands in front of three "soldiers", only one of whom, however, is preserved and of him only the head shows, his body being covered by some sort of shield or cloak. Here is indeed a military scene, and it dates between 1550 and 1500 B.C. Some people, however, have seen in the stance and features of the figures a scene of children at play: it certainly does give that impression. Even so, children do not play at soldiers who have never seen one.

The commonsense comment is surely that no Bronze Age ruler would be without his bodyguard, his small army, and that if he had such his country could still be an essentially peaceful country. The remains of bronze spears have indeed been found, and they do not all date from the period of the use of Linear B. There is also the fact that Knossos ruled the seas, indeed must have done so if she were to remain at peace at home. We have already noted that there is no evidence for imagining a large and efficient standing fleet. But the sailors must have been around, and have sometimes had to use their arms. All the difference in the world exists between keeping the peace at home and becoming a militant and empire-building nation.

There is evidence, slender evidence, that towards the end the Minoan rulers did do just this: become militant and empire-minded. They may have been forced to do so, as Rome was forced to do so, though one would imagine, from the contrasting character of the two peoples, less willingly so. As the Romans knew only too well, there are always the jealous "barbarians" without; and occupation of a land may be necessary to protect trade, or at least may seem so.

Legend here gives its support, as even do the ancient historians — Herodotus and Thucydides of Greece and Diodorus Siculus of Rome — all referring to Crete as a one-time power in the Mediterranean. Part of the legend of King Minos is that, pursuing Daedalus, who had incurred his wrath, he landed in Sicily, and founded a city there, "Minoa", before he was killed by treachery. The wrath in question refers us back to earlier conquering expeditions of King Minos. Daedalus, it will be remembered, had furnished the clue that enabled Theseus to suceed and to elope with Ariadne, Theseus being one of the seven youths and maidens who went to Greece as sacrificial tribute. And the tribute had been enforced after a punitive expedition on the part of Minos to avenge the murder of his son in the land of Greece: both Megara and Athens had felt the might of his arms. At Athens, it is interesting to note, he was not wholly successful, having to enlist the aid of Zeus and that scourge that was always considered God-given, the plague. In Sicily he was the reverse of successful, for there he met his end; Herodotus also speaks of an abortive five-year siege after his death.

We come now to earthquake. Seismologists think that Crete may have suffered in the past at the average rate of as much as three serious shocks a century. About 1700 B.C. the palace of Knossos was ruined and after a while rebuilt in greater splendour. There is the known fact that at some time in the mid-second millennium B.C. the cycladic island of Thera (modern Santorin) suffered a quite catastrophic volcanic eruption that must have caused tidal waves and probably ensuing earthquakes over a surrounding area that would certainly include Crete. The date of this disaster to Thera, unfortunately, cannot be determined with accuracy. It is thought to have occurred round about 1500 B.C.

The Chieftain's Cup, from Hagia Triada

Here, then, is the probability. Minoan Crete had weakened herself. Earthquake and the efforts made to rebuild even more grandly after earthquake, coupled with ambition or necessity that had caused her rulers to seek conquest overseas, weakened her and made her at last vulnerable. The Mycenaeans, the up-and-coming power, had taken advantage of that weakness, but not at this stage by violence. Around 1450, by means of what other pressures is unknown, a Mycenaean dynasty took over control of Minoan Crete. Or at least they took over control of Knossos, and he who had control of Knossos probably had control of Crete.

The Mycenaean aristocrats were good learners and even at times kindly as well as efficient rulers. Prosperity continued in Crete and, as we have said, was even perhaps increased. The accounting script was improved and adapted to the Greek language. The court life continued, shifting only to a more military aspect, a horse-and-chariot consciousness, the pretty ladies perhaps trying to be even prettier for the benefit of the handsome men at the reins. No doubt the mass of peasants noticed practically no difference at all: possibly a better price on the whole for their wool and figs and olives, but coupled with an increased arrogance from the aristocratic buyers.

Then, after only those fifty years of Greek dynastic interference, at or about 1400 B.C. — and within a few years this date is not in dispute — a real though not quite irretrievable physical disaster fell upon Knossos and Phaistos, and Mallia, and upon many a minor palace and major villa as well.

We come back at last to the legend of Theseus and Ariadne, only referred to so far in passing.

Let us recount it shortly. Theseus, successful and adventurous son of King Aegeus of Athens, elected to become one of the yearly (or, as some say, nine-yearly) sacrifice of seven youths and seven maidens that had to be sent to King Minos. Arriving at the port of Knossos, Theseus first proved his prowess and his command of the goodwill of the god Poseidon by retrieving from the sea the gold ring that King Minos scornfully flung there, bringing up with him for good measure a crown presented to him by Poseidon's wife. Ariadne, daughter of the king, promptly fell in love with him. The ordained fate of Theseus, along with his thirteen companions, was to be thrown to the horrible bull-headed Minotaur, the product of his mother's unnatural mating with a bull, who lived in a den at the centre of the labyrinth. Ariadne, however, had other ideas. She presented her lover with a magic sword and a magic clue-box, which would unwind its thread before him and lead him both into the presence of the Minotaur and also safely out of the labyrinth again. Theseus accomplished his heroic deed, and departed, not only with his rescued companions but with Ariadne. Ariadne, however, he left on the way home, on the island of Naxos, where in due course she became the bride of the god Dionysus. On his return to Athens, Theseus forgot to hoist the white sail which was the agreed signal of success, and his father in despair cast himself into the Aegean, thus giving his name to a sea and conventionally vacating his throne for his son. Later Theseus, as King of Athens, married Ariadne's younger sister Phaedra.

There are two things to avoid in dealing with a legend. One is to make too much of it, the other is to disbelieve it entirely: a middle course is required. Here is a story that came down to the Greeks through many centuries, accreting to itself magic highlights as it went and reflecting the predilections and remembered fears of those who told it.

The Greeks who came to Minoan Crete—and as we shall see they came a second time—must have been tremendously impressed with the labyrinthine palace. They must have been equally impressed with the Cretan bull and the Cretans' worship of the bull. Perhaps they were suddenly, traumatically shocked by the sight of someone ritually wearing a bull-mask or head-dress. They were also recounting obviously some sort of Greek success—a raid, a foray, even an invasion, but in any case a flouting of the power of the great Minos. In the incident of Theseus turning over Ariadne to the love of the god Dionysus they were remembering no doubt the dedicated holiness of the Cretan king's daughter. In Theseus's subsequent marriage to Phaedra they were remembering, possibly, a dynastic arrangement with the rulers of Knossos such as we have already supposed. As for the intended fate of the seven youths and seven maidens, it is a tempting translation to say that they were destined for the bullring. If this were true it would indeed represent a sad falling off and decadence on the part of the Minoans, that no longer their elite, with *noblesse oblige,* nor even the naturally brave, were willing to take on the dangerous but heroic job, or at least not in sufficient numbers. It is certainly a possibility, however. Another possibility is that there really did exist a clue-box, that is to say a box that would let out a thread; such was discovered in an earthquake-ruined house of Knossos and named half facetiously by Evans's excavators "Ariadne's clue-box". The romantically minded can make what they like of that; perhaps at least people did get lost in the mazes of the House of the Double Axe. . . .

How can we fit all this into the archaeological facts and probabilities, and so obtain the likely truth of the last few generations of the life of the Minoans? Obviously it is not easy. We will list three possibilities. One of them will take note of the criticisms and accusations of Professor L. R. Palmer which of late years have caused such a stir.

The first possibility is that the Theseus exploit represents an infiltration of the Mycenaean Greeks at about 1450 B.C. That would make it a not entirely peaceful affair, though we do get the element of dynastic arrangement with Theseus's subsequent marriage to Phaedra. It would also make the 1400 B.C. destruction of the palace not the result of foreign invasion but a natural catastrophe, or even a revolt of the native Minoans against their Mycenaean rulers.

The second possibility is that the 1400 B.C. destruction of Knossos and the other palaces *was* in fact the result of an invasion by the Greeks led by Theseus. In that case, however, we should have Greeks fighting Greeks, since for fifty years Knossos had been using the Greek-language Linear B script. The defence of this theory would be that such a possibility is by no means fantastic. The Greeks never had much of a name for unity. And the Mycenaean noblemen, who loved nothing better than a military adventure, who according to Homer thought the sobriquet "Sacker of Cities" highly honourable, were quite capable of fighting among themselves.

The third possibility would again allow the 1400 B.C. destruction of the Minoan palaces to be the work of Theseus but would not allow that he was fighting against other Greeks already arrived. This theory must of course assume that the presently accepted dating of the Linear B tablets discovered at Knossos is wrong. Such is exactly the assumption that Professor Palmer is maintaining. It is not the place here to set down his arguments, and any attempt at a short summary would not be likely to do justice to them. The strongest point in the argument is the unlikelihood that the almost identical Linear B writing of Knossos and of Pylos should date respectively at 1450–1400 and about 1250 B.C. The Pylos date cannot seriously be questioned; therefore, the argument runs, the Knossos date must be wrong, should in fact tally pretty closely with the Pylos.

This dispute, as to the correct date of the Knossos Linear B tablets, continues. Professor Palmer accuses Sir Arthur Evans of carelessness and inaccuracy. Nearly everyone else hotly defends him. A definite answer cannot possibly be given until further factual evidence is obtained, ideally the discovery of some more Linear B tablets in Crete, in a position that will enable a certain dating to be given to them. The position remains at the moment that the concensus of opinion is against Palmer. That the two sets of tablets, at Pylos and Knossos, should date at a difference of 150 years or more is indeed extraordinary but does nevertheless seem to be a fact. Recent discoveries at Greek Thebes (as reported in the *Illustrated London News* of 5 December 1964) of Linear B tablets of intermediate date do support the strange fact—and weaken Palmer's case.*

We come back to the lives of the Minoans. It would be a dismal affair if, in becoming immersed in the problem that they have set us we forgot that in the process of doing so they gave themselves, in one word, hell.

We will, then, be humanitarian and not too scientific. Knossos showed to those who denuded its ruins signs of chaos and terror; it also showed smoke-blackened stones, the smoke that caused it having drifted from the south, which is the way the wind blows in the spring. On a spring day then, it is likely, in the last years of what we call the fifteenth century B.C., Knossos fell: it may have been to the swords of Mycenaean swashbucklers, to the anger and more primitive weapons of peasants revolting, or to the terrible onslaught of the bellowing underground bull. Here is the description of J. D. S. Pendlebury, often quoted but not outdated.

> The final scene takes place in the most dramatic room ever excavated — the Throne Room. It was found in a state of complete confusion. A great oil jar lay overturned in one corner, ritual vessels were in the act of being used when disaster came. It looks as if the king had been hurried here to undergo too late some last ceremony in the hopes of saving the people. Theseus and the Minotaur! Dare we believe that he wore the mask of the bull?

Theseus or no Theseus at this time, there might well have been a bull-masked ceremony of propitiation as fire and terror swept through the corridors of the vast, sprawling palace of Knossos.

---

* The interested reader is referred to the second and revised edition of Palmer's *Mycenaeans and Minoans* (London, 1965), a closely reasoned book. This dispute of the experts must naturally disconcert the general reader. But this at least may be said. If Professor Palmer were to be proved right, our assessment in particular of the impact of the Mycenaeans upon the Minoans would have to be revised, and we should have to credit the Minoans with a longer span of unmolested greatness. But we should not have to revise our conception of that greatness.

Chapter Eleven

TWILIGHT

Whether Knossos and the other palaces and cities were sacked or destroyed by nature, whether the scenes were Pompeiian or more like those of Troy from which Aeneas fled, the end of Minoan Crete was not yet. There ensued, as it were, a slow fading; some prehistorians would put its end at 1200 B.C., some 1100, some as late as 1050. Minoan Crete then became Crete of the Dorian Greeks, Bronze Age Crete became Iron Age Crete. The change, one cannot help feeling, was not for the better.

These last centuries of the Minoans we need by no means think of as wholly miserable. The glory had departed, yes; but the island's fertility was still there, and surely still there much of the island people's courage. The Minoans had recovered from earthquake disaster before, and could do so again. This time, however, circumstances would be too much for them and the recovery would never be complete. Times were different now, and men as well as nature were disturbed. A full recovery was impossible. The glitter, even the great wealth, would not return.

What did seem to return was piety, an increased piety. The typical archaeological find for this period (Late Minoan III) is a clay figure with upraised arms in worship, or possibly blessing. One such figure also shows doves and the "horns of consecration" on her head—this upraised arm position is, incidentally, much like the conventionalized "horns of consecration", so that just possibly the latter could represent a religious stance and not the horns of a bull.

What is striking about this and all other finds of this period is their crudity. It is amateur art, home-made art, almost a return to neolithic art. What has happened to the real artists and craftsmen of Crete? The answer lies in the palaces and tombs of mainland Greece's Mycenae and Tiryns and Orchomenos and Pylos and Vaphio. To Greece the artists had fled, where was still the wealthy patron who would employ them. There they continued to produce their metalwork, their frescoes, their seals, their ivory figures. Skill had not deserted them, nor did they change their style; but their new masters often asked for new and different objects to look upon or subjects to portray: the sword, the helmeted chieftain, the scenes of combat or of the chase. There is even a trace of Minoan art at the short-lived capital city of the "rebel" Egyptian pharaoh Akhnaten, though this is as it were at one remove, being Mycenaean ware and not Minoan; it would be pleasant to think, however, as is at least possible, that the liveliness and naturalness of Akhnaten's art owed something to the Minoan artist.

As for the great majority of Minoans left behind in Crete, there are signs that immedi-

Late Minoan clay figure with arms upraised in worship and with doves and "horns of consecration" on her head

ately after the widespread disaster they fled to the hills, where villages and small towns dating from these times have been unearthed. Slowly they returned, at least to the cities and in a few instances to the palaces, Knossos in particular. Arthur Evans calls them squatters: they do not rebuild so much as patch up. One imagines the equivalent of a modern shanty town, with wood, even half-charred wood, for corrugated iron and a crude clay shrine for the television set stuck on top of a crate. Perhaps it was not as bad as that; Professor Palmer, in support of his theory that now were the times of the use of Linear B in Knossos, would certainly have us think so, and perhaps he is right.

The fundamental truth of these times is that the Minoans were now subservient to the Mycenaeans. These centuries, the fourteenth and thirteenth, are the centuries of the culmination of Mycenaean greatness; and, as the archaeologists from Schliemann onwards have shown us, it was a much more truly impressive greatness than could ever have been guessed at by the most attentive or optimistic reader of Homer.

Another truth is that the Mycenaeans were playing themselves out. They had the misfortune to live in disturbed times, though they themselves no doubt did not fail to contribute to the disturbance. The worlds of the Mediterranean and the Near East were on the move. They were irremediably disturbed.

One general cause of change and disturbance was the gradual introduction of the use of iron. Iron is a much more plentiful metal than copper or tin, and once the more difficult process of extracting it from its ore had been mastered, it produced not only better weapons but cheaper weapons: as Gordon Childe has said, iron helped to democratize war, and the noble and richly armed bronze-clad warrior was on his way out.

A second cause of this general disturbance, in the Aegean at least and perhaps also in Asia Minor, was the onrush of yet another wave of Aryan-speaking tribes from the north. Just as the Mycenaeans may have taken their opportunity to infiltrate into or attack a Minoan Crete that had overreached itself, so now a new and thoroughly uncivilized Greek tribe, the Dorians, paid the Mycenaeans with their own coin. The end comes virtually with the end of Troy. That event dates at about 1190 B.C. It was the Mycenaeans' final fling—and if it took them ten years to accomplish their task, as Homer says, then it was a somewhat mismanaged and inefficient fling. The Minoans, says Homer, were among those allies of the great but foolish Agamemnon who sent a contingent to the fight.

With that splendid and futile gesture we may well leave the Minoans—adding simply that they suffered, with Mycenae, from a perhaps slow but nevertheless quite ruthless and complete taking over by the Dorian Greeks.

Even at this sad ending they were, it may be said, nevertheless on the side of the angels—the classical angels, if there are such beings. For in attending at the funeral of the Mycenaeans and the budding success of the new Dorian Greeks, though they were helping to create a Dark Age of three or four centuries they were also making way for the emergence of the great classical age of Greece.

The Dorians learnt from the Mycenaeans and the Mycenaeans learnt from the Minoans. Much in the process would be forgotten—including the Linear B script, and that was probably all to the good. But much would be inherited—to become finally the heritage of modern Europe.

How to sail the seas with success, how to trade and to make things with which to trade, how in particular to make beautiful things, both to sell and to keep. How to live a hardy life, and indulge in games and feats of skill and strength. How to live comfortably and graciously (which is not the same thing as living lazily and gluttonously), how to create cities and live as individuals within them. How to be happy and not too afraid of the powers of evil or of death. These skills are the heritage bequeathed by those very lively people of Bronze Age Crete, whose true name we do not know but whom we shall always call the Minoans.

BIBLIOGRAPHY

A book that cannot help but make a profound impression, both from its text and its illustrations, is *Crete and Mycenae* (London, 1960) by Spyridon Marinatos, with photographs by Max Hirmer. Another fine book finely illustrated is *Crete and Early Greece* by Friedrich Matz (London, 1962).

The great source book is of course *The Palace of Minos* by Sir Arthur Evans (London, 1921–35) — let no one expect it to be dull or overwhelming. Two other books written by actual excavators are *The Archaeology of Crete* by J. D. S. Pendlebury (London, 1939), and *Crete, the Forerunner of Greece,* by C. H. and H. B. Hawes (New York, 1909).

A comprehensive though inexpensive book is *Prehistoric Crete* by R. W. Hutchinson, published as a Penguin paperback. The palaces are dealt with comprehensively by James Walter Graham in *The Palaces of Crete* (Princeton, N.J., 1962).

The Bull of Minos, by Leonard Cottrell (London, 1953), gives a most readable account both of Sir Arthur Evans's work in Crete and of Heinrich Schliemann's in Troy and Mycenae.

The books for those interested in the Linear B script are *Documents in Mycenaean Greek* by Michael Ventris and John Chadwick (Cambridge, 1956), and *Mycenaeans and Minoans* by Leonard R. Palmer (London, second revised edition, 1965).

ACKNOWLEDGEMENTS

For permission to reproduce copyright illustrations, grateful acknowledgements are made to:

Ashmolean Museum, Oxford, pages 15, 18, 32, 56, 60, 66, 91, 92, 94, 97, 99 *top right,* 103, 104 and 105

British Museum, page 58 *right*

Faculty of Classics, University of Cambridge, page 87

Hirmer Verlag, pages 13, 14, 22, 30, 35, 38, 45, 49 *bottom,* 53, 69, 72, 75, 76, 93, 95, 99 *top left and bottom,* 101, 102, 107, 112, 116, 121, 122, 123, 130 and 135

Picturepoint, page 41

The endpapers are from a photograph by Alison Frantz.

Plate 9 and the picture on page 67 are reproduced by kind permission of the literary executors of the late Sir Arthur Evans.

The drawings on pages 23, 24, 25, 26, 27, 28, 29, 39, 40, 43, 46, 49 *top,* 54, 57, 58 *left,* 59, 71, 73, 74, 77, 79, 80, 88, 109, 115 and 128 are by Sally Mellersh.

The passages from *Crete and Mycenae* by Spyridon Marinatos are quoted by kind permission of Thames & Hudson Limited.

INDEX

The page numbers in *italic type* indicate illustrations